Multimodal Conversation Analysis and Interpretative Phenomenological Analysis

This book presents the methodological framework of combining Multimodal Conversation Analysis (MCA) with Interpretative Phenomenological Analysis (IPA) to interpretively analyse translanguaging practices in educational contexts.

Beginning with an overview of the three uses of translanguaging—translanguaging as a theory of language, as a pedagogical practice, and as an analytical perspective—the book goes on to critically examine the different methodological approaches for analysing translanguaging practices in multilingual classroom interactions. It explains how MCA and IPA are useful methodologies for understanding how and why translanguaging practices are constructed by participants in the classroom and discusses types of data collected and data collection procedures. The author, Kevin W. H. Tai, shows how combining these approaches enables researchers to study how translanguaging practices are constructed in multilingual classrooms and how teachers make sense of their own translanguaging practices at particular moments of classroom interaction.

This detailed and concise guide is indispensable for students, practitioners, policymakers, and researchers from across the globe, particularly those working in the fields of applied linguistics and language education.

Kevin W. H. Tai is Assistant Professor of English Language Education at the Faculty of Education in The University of Hong Kong and an Honorary Research Fellow at IOE, UCL's Faculty of Education and Society in University College London (UCL), UK. He is Associate Editor of *The Language Learning Journal* and Assistant Editor of the *International Journal of Bilingual Education and Bilingualism*.

Qualitative and Visual Methodologies in Educational Research

Series Editors: Rita Chawla-Duggan and Simon Hayhoe, University of Bath, UK

We are increasingly living in an era where students and researchers are under severe time pressures, whilst the amount of research topics, methodologies, data collection methods, and ethical questions continue to grow. The *Qualitative and Visual Methodologies in Educational Research* series provides concise, accessible texts that take account of the methodological issues that emerge out of researching educational issues. They are ideal reading for all those designing and implementing unfamiliar qualitative research methods, from undergraduates to the most experienced researchers.

Books in the series:

- Are compact, comprehensive works, to appeal to final year undergraduates and early career postgraduates, at masters and doctoral level—both PhD and EdD. These works can also be easily read and digested by emerging, early career researchers, or raise issues applicable to experienced researchers who are keeping up with their field.
- Reflect on a single methodological problem per volume. In particular, the titles examine data analysis, research design, access, sampling, ethics, the role of theory, and how fieldwork is experienced in real time.
- Have chapters that discuss the context of education, teaching, and learning, and so can include a psychological as well as social and cultural understanding of teaching and learning in nontraditional or nonformal as well as formal settings.
- Include discussions that engage critically with ontological and epistemological debates underpinning the choice of qualitative or visual methodologies in educational research.

The *Qualitative and Visual Methodologies in Educational Research* series includes books which stimulate ideas and help the reader design important and insightful research that improves the lives of others though education, to ultimately inspire the development of qualitative and visual methodologies.

Titles in the series include:

Multimodal Conversation Analysis and Interpretative Phenomenological Analysis
A Methodological Framework for Researching Translanguaging in Multilingual Classrooms
Kevin W. H. Tai

For more information about this series, please visit: https://www.routledge.com/Qualitative-and-Visual-Methodologies-in-Educational-Research/book-series/QVMER

Multimodal Conversation Analysis and Interpretative Phenomenological Analysis
A Methodological Framework for Researching Translanguaging in Multilingual Classrooms

Kevin W. H. Tai

LONDON AND NEW YORK

First published 2023
by Routledge
4 Park Square, Milton Park, Abingdon, Oxon OX14 4RN

and by Routledge
605 Third Avenue, New York, NY 10158

Routledge is an imprint of the Taylor & Francis Group, an informa business

© 2023 Kevin W. H. Tai

The right of Kevin W. H. Tai to be identified as author of this work has been asserted in accordance with sections 77 and 78 of the Copyright, Designs and Patents Act 1988.

All rights reserved. No part of this book may be reprinted or reproduced or utilised in any form or by any electronic, mechanical, or other means, now known or hereafter invented, including photocopying and recording, or in any information storage or retrieval system, without permission in writing from the publishers.

Trademark notice: Product or corporate names may be trademarks or registered trademarks, and are used only for identification and explanation without intent to infringe.

British Library Cataloguing-in-Publication Data
A catalogue record for this book is available from the British Library

ISBN: 978-1-032-39714-6 (hbk)
ISBN: 978-1-032-39715-3 (pbk)
ISBN: 978-1-003-35104-7 (ebk)

DOI: 10.4324/9781003351047

Typeset in Times New Roman
by SPi Technologies India Pvt Ltd (Straive)

Contents

List of Illustration		vi
List of Classroom Extracts		vii
About the Author		viii
1	Introduction	1
2	Methodological Approaches in Researching Translanguaging in Multilingual Classroom Settings	7
3	Multimodal Conversation Analysis for Investigating the Process of Classroom Translanguaging	33
4	Interpretative Phenomenological Analysis for Investigating the Causes of Classroom Translanguaging	52
5	Triangulating Multimodal Conversation Analysis and Interpretative Phenomenological Analysis for Researching Classroom Translanguaging: Examples from Secondary English Medium Instruction Classrooms in Hong Kong	65
6	Conclusion	106
	Appendix: Multimodal Conversation Analysis Transcription Conventions	112
	Index	114

Illustration

Figures

1.1	Continuum of different multilingual education programmes (adapted from Thompson and McKinley, 2018)	4
3.1	Lin and Wu, 2015: 304–305	43
3.2	Jakonen et al., 2018: 38	45
5.1	Combining Multimodal Conversation Analysis (MCA) with Interpretative Phenomenological Analysis (IPA)	70
5.2	Pedagogical Model for Creating Translanguaging Sub-Spaces	101

Tables

4.1	A set of relationships which can be employed to interpret the data (adapted from Smith et al., 2013: 28)	56
4.2	Stages that are involved in the IPA analysis	58
5.1	Video-stimulated-recall interview	82
5.2	Video-stimulated-recall interview	95

Classroom Extracts

Extracts 1

Part 1	76
Part 2	77
Part 3	78
Part 4	78
Part 5	79

Extracts 2

Part 1	87
Part 2	88
Part 3	89
Part 4	90
Part 5	91
Part 6	92

About the Author

Kevin W. H. Tai is Assistant Professor of English Language Education at the Faculty of Education in The University of Hong Kong and Honorary Research Fellow at IOE, UCL's Faculty of Education and Society in University College London (UCL). Additionally, he is Associate Editor of *The Language Learning Journal* (Routledge), Assistant Editor of the *International Journal of Bilingual Education and Bilingualism* (Routledge) and Managing Guest Editor of *Learning and Instruction* (Elsevier).

Kevin W. H. Tai has a PhD in Applied Linguistics from UCL, and his doctoral research was fully funded by the UK Economic and Social Research Council (ESRC). He completed his doctoral coursework in educational research at the University of Cambridge, where he was Hughes Hall Hong Kong Alumni Scholar. He holds an MSc degree in Applied Linguistics and Second Language Acquisition from the University of Oxford. His research interests include language education policy, classroom discourse, translanguaging in multilingual contexts, and qualitative research methods (particularly Multimodal Conversation Analysis, Interpretative Phenomenological Analysis, and Linguistic Ethnography). His research has appeared in international peer-reviewed journals, including *Applied Linguistics, Language Teaching Research, International Journal of Bilingual Education and Bilingualism, System, Language and Education, Linguistics and Education, Classroom Discourse, Applied Linguistics Review, and Research in Science Education.*

1 Introduction

1.1 Introduction

Translanguaging refers to the process which speakers draw on their full linguistic and semiotic resources to make meaning (Li, 2018; Ho and Li, 2019; Lin, 2019). It differs from code-switching by decentering the focus from the code to the speakers who are constructing complex destructive practices. Translanguaging aims to transcend the boundaries between different named languages and also between different modalities (e.g., speech, sign, gesture). Since translanguaging practices are complex in nature, it is necessary to have a flexible methodological framework that can integrate multiple theoretical orientations, methodologies, and data sources to understand the complexities of translanguaging practices (Li, 2018).

This book is the first book in the field of applied linguistics which presents in detail the methodological framework, namely combining Multimodal Conversation Analysis (MCA) with Interpretative Phenomenological Analysis (IPA), to interpretively analyse the translanguaging practices in educational contexts (Tai and Li, 2020, 2021a, 2021b, 2021c, 2023; Tai, 2022, 2023a, 2023b; Tai and Wong, 2022). MCA offers a detailed analysis of classroom interaction which allows researchers to get at the question of 'how' from the participants' perspectives, that is, how teachers draw on multiple linguistic, multimodal, and spatial resources to shape their pedagogical practices and how the students themselves treat these practices. Additionally, using IPA allows researchers to take an emic approach in order to explore how the teachers understand and make sense of their translanguaging practices in the classrooms. Hence, triangulating MCA and IPA affords researchers the ability to study how translanguaging practices are constructed in multilingual classrooms and how the teachers make sense of their own translanguaging practices at particular moments of the classroom interaction. This methodological approach allows researchers to go beyond doing structural analysis to identify the frequent and regular patterns. This redirects the researchers in focusing on how language users break boundaries between named languages and nonlinguistic semiotic systems in particular moments of the classroom interaction (Li, 2018, 2011).

The case study and data collection methods in this book are based on my doctoral research project on translanguaging in Hong Kong English Medium Instruction (EMI) secondary classrooms. Although this book refers to examples of research on translanguaging in EMI contexts, they are merely illustrative of the research methodology used in the doctoral project and the implementation of a model of practice and analysis. The focus of this book is the employment of both MCA and IPA in understanding translanguaging in multilingual classroom contexts, how it came into being, and how it is now used in research studies.

Therefore, it is hoped that you will gain a better understanding of how MCA and IPA can be methodologically combined together to capture the complexities of translanguaging practices in multilingual educational contexts. This, in turn, can prompt the policymakers to recognize translanguaging as an empowering tool for maximizing opportunities for students to employ their full linguistic and semiotic resources in knowledge construction. You should also understand the data collection and data analysis procedures in MCA and IPA, as well as their theoretical frameworks.

In this book, I use the term 'multilingual classroom' for referring to classroom settings with students who may speak more than one language at their disposal, who may have various linguistic and cultural backgrounds, be learning the language of instruction as a foreign language, or learning the content subjects through second language (L2) as the medium of instruction. Since the book focuses on the methodological approaches in investigating translanguaging practices in multilingual classroom contexts, it is hoped that researchers who conduct translanguaging research on linguistically and culturally diverse classrooms will benefit from reading this book. The book aims to raise the researcher's awareness of the potential of combining MCA and IPA together in understanding the capacity of translanguaging as a resource for pedagogical scaffolding and maximising both content and language learning.

1.2 Different Types of Multilingual Education Programmes

With the different variants of multilingual education programmes, scholars have attempted to identify the similarities and differences.

These educational approaches are different from each other regarding the goals, teachers' and students' profiles, historical and sociocultural contexts, educational policies, pedagogical practices, curriculum design, and the involved named languages (Cenoz et al., 2014). For example, immersion programmes originated from the Canadian immersion programmes, which aim to facilitate the process of learning French, one of the official languages in Canada, for Anglophone children (Lambert and Tucker, 1972). Content and Language Integrated Learning (CLIL), a label which is typically used in Europe, is defined as 'an educational approach in which various language-supportive methodologies are used which lead to a dual-focused form of instruction where attention is given both to the language and to the content' (Coyle et al., 2010: 3). According to Marsh (2002), CLIL programmes should have a dual focus on both language and content, even though the proportion is 90 percent versus 10 percent. Such a flexible definition can lead to a wide variation in CLIL instruction. Content-Based Immersion (CBI), on the other hand, refers to 'instructional approaches that make a dual though not necessarily equal, commitment to language and content-learning objectives' (Stoller, 2008: 59). Moreover, EMI has been defined in various ways in the literature, but Macaro (2018) offers a succinct definition that reflects its specific features. He states that EMI is 'the use of the English language to teach academic subjects (other than English itself) in countries and jurisdictions where the L1 of the majority of the population is not English' (p. 19). Although they come from different names and different practices, such as EMI, CLIL and CBI, they do share a common feature which involves the use of the students' L2 as the medium of instruction when teaching and learning content subjects. It is also worth noting that English as the Specific Purpose (ESP) and English as the Academic Purpose (EAP) are classes where the English language is taught as an individual subject itself. In theory, other variants, such as CLIL, CBI, and immersion education, allow schools or teachers to select any language as the medium of instruction. Nevertheless, it has been observed that English is predominantly the language used, particularly in the European CLIL (Dalton-Puffer et al., 2010; Macaro, 2018). Figure 1.1 demonstrates the continuum of content and language learning aims in different educational programmes. In the continuum, the differences lie in whether the difference is on content or language per se. Such differences can be noticed in the programme's learning outcomes, pedagogical practices, and assessment of the learning outcomes. For example, the emphasis of EAP and ESP programmes is placed on the language-oriented domain since students will learn general academic language skills and

4 *Introduction*

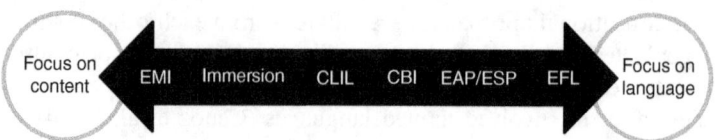

Figure 1.1 Continuum of different multilingual education programmes.
(adapted from Thompson and McKinley, 2018)

will be assessed on their English proficiency. Alternatively, EMI programmes are placed towards the content-oriented domain since EMI has content learning as the main goal, and English acquisition is secondary. Students are assessed on their content knowledge in English (i.e., L2), rather than their English proficiency.

1.3 The Structure of the Book

The book begins with discussing the concept of translanguaging from the perspectives of bi/multilingual pedagogy, languaging, multimodality and multilingualism. Chapter 2 also reviews relevant literature on translanguaging as a pedagogical resource in multilingual classrooms. It then discusses the nature and guiding principles of classroom translanguaging research and invite readers to critically examine the different methodological approaches for analysing translanguaging practices in classroom interactions.

The third and fourth chapters explain why MCA and IPA are considered as useful methodologies for understanding how and why translanguaging practices are constructed by participants in the classroom. The chapters further explain the data collection procedures and the types of data that will be collected, analysing the data. These types of data include classroom video recordings and video-stimulated-recall interviews.

The fifth chapter refers to a doctoral research project that was conducted by me in order to illustrate how MCA and IPA can be triangulated for demonstrating the complexity of classroom participants' translanguaging practices. It also focuses on the methodological issues that researchers will encounter when using MCA and IPA for analysing their research findings. The final chapter explains the methodological implications to research in applied linguistics and future directions for research.

By exploring these issues, this book aims to offer methodological implications to the field of applied linguistics. This book is indispensable for researchers, education policymakers, higher education educators, as well as undergraduate and postgraduate students studying in the fields of applied linguistics, language education, and teaching English to speakers of other languages.

References

Cenoz, J., F. Genesee, and D. Gorter. 2014. 'Critical analysis of CLIL: Taking stock and looking forward'. *Applied Linguistics* 35 (3): 243–262.

Coyle, D., P. Hood, and D. Marsh. 2010. *CLIL: Content and language integrated learning*. Cambridge: Cambridge University Press.

Dalton-Puffer, C., T. Nikula, and U. Smit. 2010. 'Language use and language learning in CLIL: current findings and contentious issues'. In C. Dalton-Puffer, T. Nikula, and U. Smit (eds.), *Language use and language learning in CLIL classrooms*. Amsterdam, the Netherlands: John Benjamins, 279–291.

Ho, W. Y. J. and W. Li. 2019. 'Mobilising learning: A translanguaging view'. *Chinese Semiotic Studies* 15 (4): 533–559.

Lambert, W. E. and G. R. Tucker. 1972. *The bilingual education of children: The St. Lambert experiment*. Rowley, MA: Newbury House.

Li, W. 2011. 'Moment analysis and translanguaging space: Discursive construction of identities by multilingual Chinese youth in Britain'. *Journal of Pragmatics* 43: 1222–1235.

Li, W. 2018. 'Translanguaging as a practical theory of language'. *Applied Linguistics* 39: 9–30.

Lin, A. M. Y. 2019. 'Theories of translanguaging and trans-semiotising: Implications for content-based education classrooms'. *International Journal of Bilingual Education and Bilingualism* 22 (1): 5–16.

Macaro, E. 2018. *English medium instruction*. Oxford: Oxford University Press.

Marsh, D. 2002. *CLIL/EMILE the European dimension*. Finland: University of Jyvaskyla.

Stoller, F. L. 2008. 'Content-based instruction'. In N. Van Deusen-Scholl and N. H. Hornberger (eds.), *Encyclopedia of language and education. Vol. 4: Second and foreign language education*. New York: Springer.

Tai, K. W. H. 2022. 'A translanguaging perspective on teacher contingency in Hong Kong English medium instruction history classrooms'. *Applied Linguistics*. Epub ahead of print. https://doi.org/10.1093/applin/amac039

Tai, K. W. H. 2023a. 'Cross-curricular connection in an Hong Kong English medium instruction western history classroom: A translanguaging view'. *Language and Education*. Epub ahead of print. https://doi.org/10.1080/09500782.2023.2174379

Tai, K. W. H. 2023b. 'Managing classroom misbehaviours in the Hong Kong English medium instruction secondary classrooms: A translanguaging perspective'. *System* 113: 1–15.

Tai, K. W. H. and W. Li. 2020. 'Bringing the outside in: Connecting students' out-of-school knowledge and experience through translanguaging in Hong Kong English medium instruction mathematics classes'. *System* 95: 1–32.

Tai, K. W. H. and W. Li. 2021a. 'Constructing playful talk through translanguaging in the English medium instruction mathematics classrooms'. *Applied Linguistics* 42 (4): 607–640.

Tai, K. W. H. and W. Li. 2021b. 'Co-learning in Hong Kong English medium instruction mathematics secondary classrooms: A translanguaging perspective'. *Language and Education* 35 (3): 241–267.

Tai, K. W. H. and W. Li. 2021c. 'The affordances of iPad for constructing a technology-mediated space in Hong Kong English medium instruction secondary classrooms: A translanguaging view'. *Language Teaching Research*. Epub ahead of print. https://doi.org/10.1177/13621688211027851

Tai, K. W. H. and C. Y. Wong. 2022. 'Empowering students through the construction of a translanguaging space in an English as a first language classroom'. *Applied Linguistics*. Epub ahead of print. https://doi.org/10.1093/applin/amac069

Tai, K. W. H. and W. Li. 2023. 'Embodied enactment of a hypothetical scenario in an English medium instruction secondary mathematics classroom: A translanguaging approach'. *Language Teaching Research*. Epub ahead of print. https://doi.org/10.1177/13621688231152858

Thompson, G. and J. McKinley. 2018. 'Integration of content and language learning'. In J. I. Liontas, M. DelliCarpini, and S. Abrar-ul-Hassan (eds.), *TESOL encyclopedia of English language teaching* (1st ed.). Hoboken, NJ: Wiley.

2 Methodological Approaches in Researching Translanguaging in Multilingual Classroom Settings

2.1 Translanguaging: Transforming Boundaries

2.1.1 Translanguaging as a Pedagogical Practice

The term 'translanguaging' was first coined by Williams (1994) in the context of Welsh bilingual classrooms in reference to the deliberate alternation between languages for receptive or productive purposes, which is reflected in the practice of reading and discussing a topic in one language and then writing about it in another in Welsh revitalisation programmes. Here, the alternation between languages is not spontaneous but rather strategic and deliberate, involving 'using one language to reinforce the other in order to increase understanding and in order to augment the pupil's ability in both languages' (Williams, 2002: 40). In other words, it aims to employ the stronger language to help learners to develop the weaker language in order to contribute to the balanced development of the student's two languages. Whilst translanguaging promotes the flexible use of multiple languages and other meaning-making resources, it seems to go against the basic premise of monolingual education policy, such as English Medium Instruction (EMI). The reality though is that in many if not all EMI classes, the use of languages other than English is actually very common. This is similar in many ways to the situation that Williams (1994) observes in the Welsh-medium classes where the teacher, following the school policy, tries to teach in Welsh only, but most pupils respond in English. Rather than seeing it as a barrier to revitalising Welsh, Williams views translanguaging as a way to realise and maximise the pupils' learning potential. Williams (1994) in the original conception wants to advocate a translanguaging pedagogy in order to assist learners in scaffolding one language with another. The term 'scaffolding' means that the 'expert' offers assistance to the novice through supportive dialogue to allow them to undertake tasks that they cannot manage

DOI: 10.4324/9781003351047-2

to complete alone (Lantolf and Aljaafreh, 1996). Although there are studies on the deployment of scaffolding techniques by teachers in multilingual classrooms, a lot of them pay attention to the teacher's use of the target language for scaffolding students' language learning in the classrooms (e.g., Donato, 1994).

However, recent translanguaging literature has paid attention to teachers' deployment of multiple linguistic resources for scaffolding. The findings of the studies (e.g., Hornberger and Link, 2012; Li, 2014; Lin and He, 2017) typically indicate that the teachers encourage students to draw on their multiple repertoires in the classroom, which consequently can facilitate the students' development of multilingualism. According to García and Li (2014: 3), the 'trans' prefix in translanguaging refers to the following aspects of language and education:

1 'trans-system and trans-spaces, in which translanguaging is going between and beyond socially constructed languages, structures and practices;
2 transformative nature of translanguaging, as traditional understandings of language practices are generated, this leads to the emergence of different discourses and voices that have been disregarded.
3 trans-disciplinary consequences of language analysis, offering a tool for understanding not only the nature of the language practices but also other aspects of socialisations, human cognition, learning, social relations and structures.'

Later expansions and theorisations of the notion have emphasized the potentially transformative nature of translanguaging for multilinguals to bring in different sociocultural dimensions, including the speakers' social identities, life histories, beliefs, and their knowledge of the wider institutional environment, as resources in the process of meaning-making (García and Li, 2014). García and Li (2014) propose that translanguaging practices are transformative as they have the potential to remove the hierarchy of languages in a society that is seen as more valuable than the others. They argue that translanguaging is viewed as a new language practice which allows the flow of fluid discourses in a different social, cultural, and political context and provides a voice to the speaker's linguistic identities that have been suppressed within the fixed linguistic ideology adopted by nation-states. In this way, translanguaging challenges the existing dichotomy of separating languages into first language (L1), L2, or Lx. Translanguaging is concerned with the entire repertoire of speakers instead of the structural knowledge of particular languages separately. Hence, translanguaging encourages teachers and students to deploy their available multilingual and multimodal resources as a way to challenge the traditional configurations, categories, and power structures; equalise the hierarchy of languages in the classrooms; and allow students' full participation in constructing new meanings and new configurations of language practices. This can potentially give voice to students who are silenced by the monolingual policy in multilingual classrooms. Hence, translanguaging can be a way for promoting equity and social justice.

Studies have illustrated that translanguaging is not only a multilingual and multimodal practice, but it can offer pedagogical and interpersonal functions in the classrooms (Cenoz and Gorter, 2011; Allard, 2017). It plays a role in deepening students' understanding of the curricular content, establishing students' identity positions, promoting inclusion and students' participation in the classrooms, preventing communication breakdown, and maintaining fluency and meaning-based interactions (Creese and Blackledge, 2010; Lewis et al., 2012; Palmer et al., 2014; Tai, 2022a). It can also provide teachers and students the options to develop their 'linguistic security and identity investment' (García, 2009: 157) and offer examples of 'dynamic bilingualism' when teachers draw on their students' linguistic and multimodal repertoires to respond to specific sociocultural contexts (Allard, 2017). Translanguaging also enables creativity and criticality in the multilingual users, which allow them to draw on their multiple communicative resources (Li, 2011). Furthermore, translanguaging has the potential to promote social justice since it eradicates the L1/L2 dichotomisation, challenges the existing hierarchies of different 'languages', and 'liberates the voices' of multilingual students (García and Leiva, 2014). Several studies have demonstrated that translanguaging can lead to students' uptake of content knowledge (Licona, 2015) and improve students' language proficiency and build rapport (García et al., 2012). The translanguaging literature indicates that translanguaging has transformative effects on pedagogy and students' development of multilingualism, as illustrated in the next section.

2.1.2 Translanguaging as a Theory of Language

In this section, I will explain how the concept of translanguaging as a theory of language is informed by the work on 'languaging' from the sociocultural perspective and ecological psychology perspective, and the concepts of multimodality and multilingualism. This section will also explain how translanguaging as a theory of language can inform our understanding of the complexity of the creative and dynamic practices language users engage in with multiple linguistic and semiotic resources.

2.1.2.1 The Sociocultural Perspective of Languaging

Under the sociocultural perspective, knowledge is constructed through social interactions where learners bring into relevance their sociocultural histories and communicative resources (Vygotsky, 1978). García (2009) notes that an individual's use of language is affected by social, cultural, political, and economic situations. Therefore, meaning-making processes are not the same in various sociocultural contexts. Individuals' literacy practices are culturally determined and are employed for particular cultural and communicative purposes. Moreover, language should not be characterised by systematicity since speakers constantly change their use of language according to different social contexts.

Extending this concept, Swain (2006: 98) introduces the term 'languaging' as 'the process of making meaning and shaping knowledge and experience through language'. It is also linked to Becker's (1991) attempt to shift away from conceptualising language as a noun that has been accomplished to language as a verb or an ongoing process. As learners employ language for making meaning and problem-solving in interaction, language becomes the tool which allows speakers to construct the idea that they are hoping to convey. Swain (2006: 97) argues that 'language serves as a vehicle through which thinking is articulated and transformed into an artefactual form'. This relates to the internalisation process which entails the learners externalising their thoughts through social interactions and then allowing learners to reflect upon these externalisations in order to make refinements accordingly. Swain (2006: 98) concludes that 'languaging about language is one of the ways we learn language'. From this perspective, it can be illustrated that Swain perceived language learning as a process rather than an outcome, which entails the negotiation and co-construction of meaning. Furthermore, Gynne and Bagga-Gupta (2015: 512) conceptualise languaging as 'ways-of-being-with-words' which emphasise the idea of 'language as a process, and product of the social activity, or a practice of interactional agency'.

All these conceptualisations of languaging share the similar idea that multilinguals strategically employ language as a tool to learn and accomplish one's communicative intentions. Swain (2006) draws on Wantanabe's (2004) analysis of an English-as-a-second-language classroom interaction and demonstrate how the learners acquire different aspects of a target language by 'talking-it-through' and specifically how the learners employ language as a mediational means to mediate their cognition in order to solve a language-related problem. Languaging, as Swain (2006: 105–106) suggests, 'mediated the students' language learning by drawing their attention to language-related problems they had, and by giving them the tools to reason with, to solutions'. This implies that languaging allows learners to develop their metalinguistic awareness so that learning becomes more explicit.

2.1.2.2 Ecological Psychology Perspective of Languaging

It is important to note that translanguaging is informed by a dialogic and distributed perspective of language. Scholars, such as Nigel Love and Paul Thibault, perceive languaging as a 'distributed and heterogenous biocultural resource that is spread over persons, environmental affordances, artefacts, cultural patterns, and values' (Thibault, 2011: 240). From their perspective, languaging refers to 'an assemblage of diverse material, biological, semiotic and cognitive properties and capacities which languaging agents orchestrate in real-time and across a diversity of timescales' (Thibault, 2017: 82). In other words, the concept of languaging rejects the idea of dividing the linguistic, paralinguistic, and extralinguistic perspectives of human communication since languaging involves the orchestration of multiple bodily resources to construct meanings. Particularly, it highlights the significance of social factors including 'feeling, experience, history, memory, subjectivity and culture', ideology and power (Li, 2018: 9).

Language is perceived as a system which originates from the speakers' situational behaviours. This perspective questions the old and established perspective of language, which assumes separate linguistic systems as pre-existing realities. The multiple linguistic and semiotic resources that speakers deploy during social interactions are seen as a product of 'first-order languaging'. Specifically, Thibault (2017: 74) notes that first-order languaging 'is an experimental flow that is enacted, maintained, and changed by the real-time activity of participants'. Based on the perspective of first-order languaging, language is social and dialogic instead of a pre-existing code. Thibault further notes that first-order languaging 'includes a whole range of bodily resources that are assembled and coordinated in languaging events together with external (extrabodily) aspects of situations' (p. 215). These multiple linguistic and multimodal resources are later codified and labelled as various named languages (often due to historical, political, or national forces). Thibault (2017: 80) employs the notion of 'second-order language' to refer to the 'reified products of first-order languaging'. That is, these different languages are considered as second-order realities rather than first-order realities. Second-order language consists of lexicogrammatical patterns which represent 'attractors—future causes—that guide and constrain first-order languaging. They are stabilised cultural patterns of longer, slower cultural timescales' (Thibault, 2011: 216). In other words, speakers are always languaging when they are engaged in meaning-making processes; that is, speakers are being led and constrained by former stabilised cultural patterns, which come under the various names of social languages, linguistic varieties, registers, and so on. From this view, languaging involves the orchestration of the whole range of bodily resources, which are multilingual, multisemiotic, multisensory, and multimodal (Li, 2018).

The languaging view on language learning perceives the novices adapting their 'bodies and brains to the languaging activity that surrounds them', and by doing so, the novices 'participate in cultural words and learn that they can get things done with others in accordance with the culturally promoted norms and values' (Thibault, 2017: 76). Thus, language learning is viewed as a process of resemiotisation (Iedema, 2003), referring to actions which allow learners to construct new meanings when they are engaging in the process of transforming a sign from one semiotic mode into another. It is also a process of participation since individuals employ multiple resources that are acquired over the course of their life trajectories through participation in different sociocultural settings (Creese and Blackledge, 2010).

Hence, the concept of languaging reinforces language as a process instead of as an object. Languaging is constantly being jointly constructed between individuals and their environments. It reconceptualises language as a 'multi-scalar organisation of processes that enables the bodily and the situated to interact with situation-transcending cultural-historical dynamics and practices' (Thibault, 2017: 78) rather than reducing language to 'linguistic objects' with corresponding formalism, including phonemes, words, and syntax. Moreover, the established notions of multilingualism, which emphasise achieving a certain level of proficiency in multiple different languages (Ellis, 2008; Rothman, 2008), have gradually been replaced by a perspective in which language users will deploy any kinds of linguistic resources that are useful and accessible to them for facilitating the meaning-making processes. Nevertheless, García and Li (2014) argue that it is necessary to have translanguaging as a notion which can better capture the complexity of the multilingual language users' language exchanges since the term 'languaging' mostly concerns the speakers' knowledge of particular structures of specific languages separately. It does not fully highlight how the multilinguals draw on their entire linguistic and multimodal repertoires to construct hybrid language practices in order to mediate their thinking and meaning-making processes (Li, 2018). By adding the 'trans' prefix to languaging, Li (2018) reinforces the idea of crossing boundaries and acknowledging fluidity and flexibility between linguistic structures, systems, and various modalities.

2.1.2.3 Translanguaging and Multimodality

Translanguaging aims to challenge the boundaries between named languages, and indeed between language varieties, which are social and political in nature (Otheguy et al., 2015; Li, 2018), which can be manipulated by the language users for strategy use in meaning-making. However, scholars (e.g., Li, 2018; Li and Ho, 2018; Ho and Li, 2019; Li, 2020; Tai and Li, 2020, 2021a, 2021b, 2021c, 2023; Tai, 2022a, 2022b, 2023a, 2023b) further conceptualise translanguaging as breaking the boundaries between linguistic and semiotic resources. By embracing the social semiotic view of multimodality, scholars problematise the ideological biases that privilege conventional linguistic codes in meaning-making. As Li (2020) argues, linguists tend to focus on linguistic aspects in communicative practices, including investigating syntax, phonology, and morphology in linguistics research. They typically pay little attention to other semiotic resources that create meaning in real-life social interactions. However, social interaction is highly multimodal, and meaning is never only conveyed through verbal utterances and writing in everyday human communication. Kress (2015) makes a similar argument, and he argues that focusing only on speech and writing in the field of applied linguistics will prevent researchers from understanding the communicative practices in contemporary society. Hence, a multimodal turn in applied linguistics is required:

> Language, as speech or writing, remains an anchoring-point in thinking and working in Applied Linguistics. Here, however, the reference-point to be discussed in multimodality. Its material resources are many and varied; they go well beyond speech and writing. 'Material' in the sense employed here refers to those phenomena which are accessible to and for engagement by the 'senses', the sensorium. All of these "material resources" impinge more or less closely on the present domain of Applied Linguistics, in ways both distinct yet closely connected.
>
> (p. 51)

There are three theoretical assumptions related to multimodality. The first assumption is that 'all interactions are multimodal' (Norris, 2004: 1). Jewitt (2009) further argues that 'multimodality describes approaches that understand communication and representation to be more than about language, and which attend to the full range of communicational forms people use [...] and the relationships between them' (p. 14). In this sense, language is only considered as one of the communicative modes, which is of equal significance with other modes, including gestures and verbal speech to contribute to meaning. The second assumption is that 'each mode in a multimodal ensemble is understood as realising different communicative work' (Jewitt, 2009: 15). Since different communication modes have different potentials for constructing meaning, each mode has its own situated meaning in a specific sociocultural context in which it is employed. Therefore, it is vital to understand that one cannot analyse social interaction holistically by just focusing on only one mode. All modes, including language, are part of a multimodal ensemble that has to be understood in its entirety (Kress, 2015). Furthermore, the third assumption is that 'people orchestrate meaning through their selection and configuration of modes' (Jewitt, 2009: 15). Although different modes perform various functions in social interactions, they do not work individually. Rather, they are orchestrated to create meanings. As argued by Jewitt (2009), different modes 'co-present' and 'cooperate' with each other to create meanings in human communication.

In recent years, there are more research studies in applied linguistics that pay attention to some form of multimodality, mostly on studying the role of gestures, to investigate the processes of L2 teaching and learning. As Smotrova and Lantolf (2013) argue, both gesture and speech form a unit that is necessary to be analysed as a whole in order to understand the role of gestures in enhancing speaking and thinking. As a result, gestures have an important role as a mediational tool in L2 learning and development, particularly in relation to vocabulary explanations (e.g., Smotrova and Lantolf, 2013; Tai and Brandt, 2018; Tai and Khabbazbashi, 2019a, 2019b), grammatical forms (e.g., Matsumoto and Dobs, 2017) and pronunciations (e.g., Tai and Poon, 2016) that are not familiar to learners. Despite such research development, Block (2014) criticises the fact that such research only focuses on one communicative mode, notably gestures, while other semiotic modes are not well-recognised. He invites researchers to 'take on board this wide range of modes more explicitly and more completely, examining how they form ensembles to communicate meaning in different contexts' (p. 70). Additionally, researchers should not only recognise multimodality as a phenomenon in everyday social interaction but should also 'embrace the potential paradigmatic shift that the notion of multimodality can bring to our understanding of communicative practices' in order to prevent producing hegemonic discourses that favour the conventional role of language (Adami, 2017: 3). As shown, multimodality has drawn researchers' attention to the multimodal means which are previously neglected in the literature. Williams's (1994) original discussion of translanguaging as a pedagogical practice has included modalities of reading, writing, listening, and speaking. As the notion has been further developed as a theoretical concept, translanguaging embraces the multimodal view that sign makers can draw on the wider repertoire of multimodal resources at their disposal to create meaning. Li (2018) further extends the notion of translanguaging as multilingual, multisemiotic, multisensory, and multimodal practices that individuals use for thinking and expressing thought. From a translanguaging perspective, this emphasises the need to look beyond the conventional conceptualisation of named languages as different codes of speech and writing, specifically, the embodied and multimodal aspects of communication.

2.1.2.4 Translanguaging and Multilingualism

A multilingual is someone who can speak more than one language. The term 'bilingualism' is often used in the literature, which typically refers to a speaker who can speak two languages. However, in the context of education, 'multilingual education' is often employed as an umbrella term which includes bilingual education (Cenoz, 2013). Moreover, the prefix 'multi-' does not simply refer to two or more languages. It has a broader meaning which refers to the 'complex linguistic interactions that cannot be enumerated' (García and Li, 2014: 3). The concept of multilingualism can be divided into two levels: individual and societal. Individual multilingualism is often used interchangeably with the term 'plurilingualism'. Plurilingualism is defined as 'the repertoire of varieties of language which many individuals use' (Council of Europe, n.d.). In this sense, 'some individuals are monolingual and some are plurilingual'. Such a perspective differs from the concept of societal multilingualism, which refers to 'the presence in a geographical area [...] of more than one variety of language [...] in such an area individuals may be monolingual, speaking only their own variety'. Although bilingualism is typically deployed at the individual level, multilingualism is normally employed at the societal level as a way to describe social groups that deploy more than two languages (García and Li, 2014).

There has been a tendency for languages to be conceptualised as separated and bounded entities. This perspective has shaped the early definition of bilingualism and multilingualism and it promotes the ideology of monolingual norm. Bi-/multilinguals are considered as deficient and lacking language competence, as implied by the notions of non-native speakers (e.g., Cook, 1999), interlanguage (Selinker, 1972), and fossilisation (Selinker, 1974). These notions refer to the multilinguals' incomplete and incorrect linguistic usage. Such a deficit perspective of bi-/multilingualism is summed up by Grosjean (1985: 468–470):

- 'Bilinguals have been described and evaluated in terms of the fluency and balance they have in their two languages
- Language skills in bilinguals have almost always been appraised in terms of monolingual standards
- The contact of the bilingual's two languages is seen as accidental and anomalous.'

The monolingual perspective of bi-/multilingualism has been criticised by sociolinguists who provide a different view of understanding bi-/multilingualism. As Blommaert et al. (2005) argue, rather than perceiving what languages the multilingual does or does not know, researchers should focus on how different languages which are known by the multilinguals can be useful resources for learning and facilitating social interactions. It is fundamental to recognise that translanguaging is concerned with the full repertoire of the language users, instead of the users' structural knowledge of particular languages (Li, 2018). The perspective that it is necessary to separate different languages in the classroom so that they will not 'interfere' with each other has received lots of criticism from applied linguists. Such a monolithic view is challenged by the dynamic bilingualism framework which

> goes beyond the idea that there are two languages that are interdependent [...] instead, it connotes one linguistic system that has features that are most often practised according to societally constructed and controlled 'languages', but other times producing new practices.
>
> (García and Li, 2014: 14)

This framework emphasises the fluidity of languages that are employed by bi-/multilinguals and that the languages are often identifiable but inseparable. It treats the bi-/multilinguals' ability to speak multiple languages as an asset instead of a hindrance affecting their learning processes. In other words, the goal of language teaching and learning should be developing students' multilingualism, instead of conforming to monolingual practices, which limits their multilingualism to two or more separate autonomous languages.

2.1.2.5 Translanguaging Space

Li (2011, 2018) theorises the notion of 'translanguaging space', which refers to the space that is created by and for translanguaging practices. As argued previously, a translanguaging perspective would interrogate the traditional divides between the linguistic, the paralinguistic, and the extralinguistic aspects of human communication as nonsensical. Nevertheless, space is not simply about its physical properties. The idea of 'socially produced' space is suggested by Lefebvre (1991), and this idea has led to subsequent scholarly work on spaces and places. The key assumption of the notion of 'socially produced space' is that space is socially constructed, and that social interaction is a social practice. Therefore, engaging in translanguaging practices can create

> a social space for the multilingual language user by bringing together different dimensions of their personal history, experience and environment; their attitude, belief, and ideology; their cognitive and physical capacity, into one coordinated and meaningful performance.
> (Li, 2011: 1223)

In other words, this translanguaging space can be transformative because such a space allows individuals to create and combine new identities, values, and practices. The notion of translanguaging space is different from other conceptualisations of language since translanguaging space aims to go beyond the boundaries between spatial and other semiotic resources as it views spatial positioning and display of objects as semiotic and socially meaningful.

Li (2018) further argues that the concept of translanguaging includes two notions which are essential to bilingual education: creativity, which refers to the ability to 'push and break boundaries between named language and between language varieties and to flout norms of behaviour' (p. 15), and criticality, which refers to the ability to use 'available evidence insightfully to inform different perspectives of cultural, social and linguistic phenomena and to challenge and express ideas through reasoned responses to situations' (p. 23). From a translanguaging lens, bi-/multilinguals are provided agency to employ various linguistic and semiotic resources creatively and critically to challenge the traditional configurations, categories, and power structures, and construct new meanings through interactions (Li, 2014; Zhu et al., 2017). As Li (2011) argues, the two notions of creativity and criticality are intrinsically connected since one cannot break boundaries (i.e., being creative) without being critical, and 'one's criticality is one's creativity' (p. 1223).

2.2 Guiding Principles of Classroom Translanguaging Research

Prior research studies on classroom discourse are mostly case studies which adopt the structural-functional linguistic analysis approach (e.g., Duarte, 2019; Probyn, 2019; Wang, 2019). It can be argued that using Discourse Analysis (DA) as a methodological approach prevents researchers from conducting a detailed, line-by-line, and fine-grained analysis of the classroom talk in order to analyse the functions of translanguaging served in the classrooms. It is noted that DA serves as an umbrella term with a focus 'on talk and text as social practice, and on the resources that are drawn on to enable practice' and the logic of DA consists of a rhetorical move and a norm (Potter, 1996: 31). The rhetorical move is related to categorization and the norm to accounts or sanctions. The central concept of DA is function. Functions are speech acts, in that functions are concerned with 'what that piece of language doing, or how the listener/reader is supposed to react' (McCarthy, 1991: 9). Additionally, particular units are related to language forms, including grammatical, lexical, and phonological ones (McCarthy, 1991). In this sense, in DA, there is a form–function mapping. Furthermore, DA favours a 'coding and category system' (Psathas, 1995: 9) which requires researchers to analyse classroom discourse in structural-functional linguistic terms. Nonetheless, the DA approach massively oversimplifies the social interaction since the interaction has to be coded as a single instructional sequence or as a single move in order to fit into the coding scheme (Seedhouse, 2004).

Wang (2019) suggests that classroom translanguaging research should adopt an ethnographic approach in order to better capture the complexities of translanguaging practices in various classroom contexts. Hence, Wang (2019) proposes five guiding principles for researchers in designing a research project on translanguaging in multilingual classrooms:

Methodological Approaches in Researching Translanguaging 19

1 Classroom translanguaging research should be descriptive instead of prescriptive in order to illuminate the ways in which classroom participants employ their full linguistic and multimodal repertoires for constructing knowledge and facilitating meaning-making processes in the classrooms.
2 Classroom translanguaging research should focus on how classroom participants employ translanguaging for achieving communicative or pedagogical purposes, rather than focusing on how the use of translanguaging fits into the structural-functional coding schemes.
3 Classroom translanguaging research should analyse both teacher-led and student-led translanguaging practices in order to capture how all classroom participants engage in translanguaging to accomplish learning and communicative objectives.
4 Classroom translanguaging research should adopt both the etic and emic perspectives in analysing the data. Doing so allows the researcher to integrate the perspectives of the classroom participants on their ways of using various linguistic and multimodal resources for meaning-making. In this book, I particularly focus on how researchers can integrate MCA and IPA, both of which methodologies focus on the emic perspective of participants, in understanding the complex multilingual and multimodal resources employed by the interactants in co-constructing meanings through translanguaging in the classrooms.
5 Classroom translanguaging research should adopt an ethnographic research design in order to afford researchers to collect different kinds of qualitative data, such as interviews, fieldnotes, audio/video data, and stimulated recalls. This, in turn, can enable researchers to triangulate different data sources for capturing the fluidity and complexity of translanguaging practices in the multilingual classrooms.

2.3 Research Studies on Translanguaging in Multilingual Classroom Contexts

2.3.1 *Using Interview Data Only to Explore Translanguaging in Multilingual Classrooms*

A growing body of work in multilingualism has revealed that translanguaging is not only a multilingual and multimodal practice, but it can offer pedagogical and interpersonal functions in multilingual classrooms (García and Li, 2014; Tai and Li, 2020; Tai, 2022b, 2023a,

2023b; Tai and Wong, 2022). For instance, Woodley (2016) illustrates how translanguaging in a highly diverse elementary classroom promotes participation. By constructing multilingual resources, including labels and signs and posters, in multiple languages; offering select home language translations; grouping students with the same L1s; and encouraging language comparisons when explaining new vocabulary items, the teacher successfully leverages students' multilingualism while communicating with his students in English. However, the findings of this study are generated from the teacher's interview data and fieldnotes. Without a detailed analysis of the classroom discourse, it is unclear how translanguaging enables inclusion in multilingual classrooms.

Similarly, Doiz and Lasagabaster (2017) examine the EMI teachers' beliefs regarding their translanguaging practices at a Spanish university. It is important to be aware that although the paper emphasises translanguaging as the research focus, the authors switch to the term 'use of L1' in their research questions. The study organises focus groups with the EMI teachers to capture and analyse their ideological discourses. A total of 13 teachers teaching economics, engineering and communication are involved in this study. The findings illustrate that the majority of the teachers believe that using L1 is detrimental to the goals of EMI and it will hinder the creation of an English-only classroom environment. Only two teachers support using languages flexibly to develop students' multilingualism. As this study does not observe the teachers' actual practices in the classrooms, the authors advocate future research to observe EMI classes in order to identify any mismatch between beliefs and practices.

2.3.2 Using Functional Discourse Analysis to Explore Translanguaging in Multilingual Classrooms

Nikula and Moore (2019) present an exploratory study of translanguaging in various secondary CLIL classroom settings (biology in Finland, technology in Spain, and history in Austria). The authors argue that they have conducted the first representative studies which explored translanguaging as a complex, fluid, and momentary practice rather than a straightforward systematic alternative of languages. The authors employ qualitative discourse analysis as the primary method to analyse the classroom talk. The analyses are similar to Lin and Wu's (2015) and Lin and He's (2017) findings that teachers and students employ translanguaging practices to fulfil different communicative intentions, including engaging in language play, orienting to pedagogical and interpersonal concerns, and delivering classroom instructions. The authors argue that their classroom findings are beyond the old-fashioned definition of translanguaging which only conceptualise translanguaging as a deliberate switch of languages for input and output in the classrooms. This study contributes to the wider literature on translanguaging by demonstrating translanguaging as a locally situated practice in various geographical CLIL contexts. Nevertheless, the study's discourse analysis of the classroom talk was simplistic and brief, which was different from Tai and Li's (2020, 2021a, 2021b, 2021c, 2023) studies where they conducted a fine-grained analysis of the classroom talk in order to analyse the functions of translanguaging served in the Hong Kong (HK) EMI classrooms.

Duarte (2019) employs sociocultural discourse analysis to analyse instances of classroom interaction in content-focused mainstream classrooms in Germany. Duarte employs a simple coding system for analysing the classroom talk, which includes the individual speech act, named languages, and different types of talk. The findings have shown that translanguaging is used to construct meaning and allow students to jointly solve the classroom tasks. For instance, translanguaging plays a role when students are making sense of the task. This includes moments when they are paraphrasing the task and describing relevant knowledge for solving the task. Translanguaging also has a role to play when students are co-constructing answers. This entails moments when they are hypothesising the answer, negotiating meaning, showing disagreement/agreement, or providing counterarguments. Nevertheless, as Duarte also acknowledges, adopting such a simplified coding system to analyse translanguaging practices creates some methodological constraints since it fails to capture the complexity of translanguaging in the classroom interactions.

2.3.3 Using an Ethnographic Approach to Explore Translanguaging in Multilingual Classrooms

One of the most pertinent studies which illustrates the creativity and criticality of the students' translanguaging is by Li (2014). Using interactional sociolinguistics, Li focuses on classroom interactions between the children and their teachers in the UK Chinese heritage language classroom, where the teacher and students both understand Chinese, and illustrates the ways in which participants switch freely between different varieties of Chinese and English and different modes of communication. Moreover, Li also demonstrates that the students bring together not only their multiple linguistic skills but also their knowledge of the social world, particularly their awareness of the history of the community to which they belong and their positions in it, as well as their attitudes and beliefs during the process of learning. Li argues that the students' creative and critical expressions of meanings in their schoolwork indicate their agency in constructing their sociocultural identities, attitudes, and values and challenges the dominance of Mandarin as the Chinese lingua franca. Such translanguaging practices go beyond pedagogy and learning and can potentially have an impact on the students' development of identity, social relationships, and values.

Lin and He (2017) conducted an ethnographic study to investigate how translanguaging is employed as a pedagogical strategy by an EMI science teacher to motivate South Asian ethnic minoritized learners from Pakistan, Nepal, and India to utilise their multilingual repertoires. Ethnographic naturalistic observations of the classroom interactions in a year 9 HK EMI science classroom are carried out to analyse the participants' translanguaging practices, and interviews are conducted to help the researchers to understand the meanings of the learners' use of Urdu phrases in the classrooms. The findings indicate that several learners employ both their knowledge from their home language expressions (Urdu) and English, as well as their body and gestures to display their understanding of the human digestive system. It is also noticeable that the teacher draws on her prior knowledge of Urdu that she has learnt previously from her learners to give the instruction in the learners' L1. The authors suggest that although the teacher and learners come from different linguistic and cultural backgrounds, their willingness to learn from other's linguistic and cultural resources have created a space for learning to take place where learners are motivated in learning the subject content through the L2 and developing their linguistic repertoires for communication. This study provides important pedagogical implications for EMI education as it offers new insights into how translanguaging can function as an effective pedagogical scaffolding strategy in EMI classrooms, particularly with learners of multilingual backgrounds, to motivate learners' content and L2 learning and facilitate the meaning-making processes. It fills in the literature gap where the participating teachers and students in most of the EMI studies shared the same L1 and uniquely explored how the teacher and students who have different L1s and cultures fulfill the classroom tasks in the same L2, English.

Although several studies (e.g. Li, 2014; Mazak and Herbas-Donoso, 2015, Woodley, 2016; Wang, 2019) have illustrated that fluid language use in the classroom could result in a beneficial impact on students' well-being, identity formation, and confidence, there is a need to consider whether translanguaging in the classroom will be effective in various classroom environments as this will 'depend on the socio-political and historical environment in which such practice is embedded and the local ecologies of schools and classrooms' (Creese and Blackledge, 2010: 107). Some educational studies (e.g., Rampton, 2006; Charalambous et al., 2016) have illustrated that translanguaging may lead to a decrease in well-being and students may not perceive translanguaging as an empowering tool to recognise linguistic diversity in society. Charalambous's et al. (2016) study is one of the few studies which illustrates how translanguaging might not be helpful in valorising linguistic hybridity in particular contexts. The ethnographic study examines how a primary school teacher introduces Turkish, which is the home language of students with Bulgarian backgrounds, in a Greek primary classroom. It is found that despite the teacher's effort in embracing her students' superdiversity and encouraging translanguaging to promote mutual understandings and maximise communication, the teacher's pedagogical practices do not encourage the suppression of Turkish-speakerness since the students fear that 'speaking Turkish' could be seen as 'being Turkish' (p. 327) as Turkishness is associated with negative historical indexicalities in Greece. The authors note that in some communities, 'discourse of conflict creates unfavourable ecologies for hybrid linguistic practices' (p. 327).

Similarly, Allard's (2017) ethnographic study examines the pedagogical functions of the teachers' translanguaging in a beginner-level ESL reading class and a beginner-level ESL science classroom in a US high school. The ESL students are Spanish speakers, and they are expected to develop their English proficiency in order to be promoted to the mainstream content classes. The ESL teachers can speak Spanish, and they both share similar Spanish proficiency. Based on the data derived from the classroom observations and teachers' interviews, the teachers' use of translanguaging is aimed to facilitate communication between low-proficiency ESL students and teachers, acknowledge students' existing linguistic repertoires, and assist students in understanding the curricular material and encourage their participation in the lessons. Nevertheless, from the students' perspectives, translanguaging is perceived as a hindrance to the students' English language development as they receive insufficient exposure to English. Due to the students' beliefs in the importance of language purity in the classroom, this weakens the power of their teachers' translanguaging, which contributes to students' low engagement with their studies, unwillingness to participate in the classrooms, and fraught student–teacher relationships. Furthermore, the school does not have a unifying language policy to celebrate multilingual diversity. Based on the ethnographic observations, the linguistic landscape in the school's areas (e.g., corridor walls) reflects the dominance of English monolingualism. Hence, although the teachers' translanguaging facilitates communication between teachers and students and affords students greater access to content, the teachers' translanguaging is not a transformative pedagogical practice due to the monolingual language ideologies reflected in students' beliefs and the absence of a coherent language policy in the school.

Therefore, it is important for translanguaging researchers not to presume that translanguaging itself can necessarily give back voice, release bilingual subjectivities, raise well-being, and ultimately transform the unequal community into a fairer world (Jaspers, 2018). This is because it is necessary to consider the local circumstances and the predominant discourses in the particular contexts before introducing specific linguistic resources in the classrooms in order to avoid resulting in negative influences on students' learning outcomes.

2.3.4 Using Mixed Methods to Explore Translanguaging in Multilingual Classroom

Makalela's (2015) mixed-method study is one of the few studies that explored the impact of translanguaging on learners' vocabulary development and oral reading proficiency. Results indicate that the translanguaging experimental group outperforms the monolingual control group in vocabulary development. However, the use of translanguaging does not influence oral reading proficiency in the experimental group. Although this study demonstrates the positive effects of translanguaging on the acquisition of an indigenous African language as an additional language in the university language classroom, the results should be interpreted with caution as there may be several confounding variables. First, there is no information given regarding fidelity to condition as it is unknown how multiple discursive resources are actually employed in the experimental group. Second, the definition of translanguaging in this study is limited; the author only focuses on the linguistic aspects of translanguaging, and throughout the paper, the author does not acknowledge the multimodal, multisensory, and multisemiotic nature of translanguaging. Third, the author designs the pre- and post-tests to assess the students' lexical and reading development. However, he does not explain whether and how he validates the pre- and post-tests in order to confirm that results of the research are valid and reliable.

Sah and Li (2022) conduct a critical discourse analysis of teachers' and students' language use in two EMI classrooms (social studies and health and population classrooms) in a multilingual public school in Nepal. The majority of the students speak the Newari language as their L1, which is an indigenous language in Nepal, and there are students from Nepali, Gurung, and Limbu speaking communities. The authors collect various data sources, including classroom observations, teacher interviews, and focus group discussions with students, to understand the ways translanguaging takes place in the EMI classrooms. The authors first conduct a quantitative analysis of the language use in the EMI classrooms, and the findings illustrate that both teachers and students employ Nepali and English variably in different classrooms. Notably, the number of Nepali words that are used by the teachers and students are more than English words in both classes in order to support students' content knowledge acquisition. The critical discourse analysis of the classroom interaction reveals that both teachers and students translanguage between English and Nepali, and this facilitates students' participation and content comprehension to a certain extent. However, the authors argue that the teachers' and students' uncritical adoption of translanguaging practices reproduces the hierarchy of named languages by privileging the national languages (e.g., Nepali) above the indigenous languages for minoritized students (e.g., Newari). It is further argued that 'unequal languaging practices create a discriminatory learning space for linguistic minoritized children' (p. 17). The study provides useful pedagogical implications for teachers and reinforces the need for EMI teachers to be critical when engaging in translanguaging and to have an awareness for promoting equal integration of minoritized languages. Nonetheless, the study only conceptualises translanguaging as switching between named languages, and it suffers from several methodological limitations. The study's critical classroom discourse analysis does not illustrate the connections between the classroom discourse and societal and cultural processes and structures (Fairclough, 1992). The authors also attempt to compare two different classrooms' language use through conducting a descriptive statistical analysis. I argue that the author could not be sure that any differences between the language uses is not a result of the characteristics of the school, teacher, or students.

Based on the review of the research studies, it is revealed that the notion of translanguaging emphasises that it does not only go between different linguistic structures, systems, and modalities but also go beyond linguistic codes. It challenges the perspective that there are boundaries between different named languages, linguistic varieties, and other communicative means. Translanguaging 'signals a trans-semiotic system with many meaning-making signs, primarily linguistic ones that combine to make up a person's semiotic repertoire' (García and Li, 2014: 42). It is a process of meaning-making which entails the speakers strategically as well as spontaneously drawing on their one linguistic and semiotic repertoire in an integrated manner without focusing on 'languages' as distinct and separate codes. This does not imply that the speaker is unaware of the structural constraints of particular named languages. In fact, Li and Ho (2018) argue that the speakers are fully aware of these facts, but the speakers are capable of deploying this knowledge to strategically achieve their communicative intentions.

2.4 Summary

In this chapter, I have given a detailed overview of the concept of translanguaging as a pedagogical practice and as a theory of language. I have explained several guiding principles of classroom translanguaging research and reviewed studies on translanguaging in bi-/multilingual classrooms.

I have argued that in order to fully understand the construction of translanguaging, researchers cannot merely rely on Conversation Analysis (CA) or DA or interview data as the primary method because external factors, such as beliefs and personal history, can be illustrated through ethnographic interviews, but they may not emerge from the CA or DA or interview data analysis directly (e.g., Antaki, 2012; see Chapter 5 for more information). Lin and He's (2017) ethnographic case study is a rare example of employing the ethnographic method to capture translanguaging practices in EMI science classrooms. It is important for more research to attempt to integrate fine-grained classroom analysis with ethnographic approach (e.g., Creese and Blackledge, 2010; Li, 2014; Allard, 2017) to study the nature of translanguaging in multilingual classrooms.

Since translanguaging practices are complex in nature (different sociocultural factors, such as personal history, life experience, identity, or beliefs, can potentially play a role in affecting our use of meaning-making resources in the process of constructing knowledge), I argue that it is necessary to have a flexible framework that can integrate multiple theoretical orientations, methodologies, and data sources to understand the complexities of translanguaging practices. Hence, I propose combining MCA along with IPA to study how translanguaging practices are constructed in multilingual classrooms and how the teachers make sense of their own translanguaging practices at particular moments of the classroom interaction (see Chapter 5). This methodological approach allows researchers to go beyond from doing structural analysis to identify the frequent and regular patterns. This redirects the researchers in focusing on how language users break boundaries between named languages and nonlinguistic semiotic systems in particular moments of the classroom interaction (Li, 2011, 2018). This echoes Li's proposal of moment analysis (see Chapter 5 for more information), which aims to investigate the spontaneous acts of creativity and criticality in everyday social interactions. Moment analysis focuses on what prompts a particular social action at a particular moment of the interaction and the consequence of the action. In this sense, the researcher is concerned with how a specific moment of the use of various linguistic, multimodal, and multisemiotic resources is being noticed or remarked upon by the participants and what may have resulted in a particular action at a specific moment of the interaction (Li and Zhu, 2013).

In the next chapter, I will provide a detailed account of MCA and explain how researchers can use MCA as a method to identify and analyse instances of translanguaging in classroom interactions.

References

Adami, E. 2017. 'Multimodality and superdiversity: Evidence for a research agenda'. *Tilburg Papers in Culture Studies* 177: 1–28.

Allard, E. 2017. 'Re-examining teacher translanguaging: An ecological perspective'. *Bilingual Research Journal* 40: 116–130.

Becker, A. L. 1991. 'Language and languaging'. *Language and Communication* 11: 33–35.

Block, D. 2014. 'Moving beyond "lingualism": Multilingual embodiment and multimodality in SLA'. In S. May (ed.), *The multilingual turn: Implications for SLA, TESOL and bilingual education*. New York; London: Routledge. 54–77.

Blommaert, J., J. Collins., and S. Slembrouck. 2005. 'Spaces of multilingualism'. *Language and Communication* 25: 197–216.

Cenoz, J. 2013. 'Bilingual and multilingual education: Overview'. In C. A. Chapelle (ed.), *The encyclopedia of applied linguistics*, (pp. 1–8). Blackwell Publishing Ltd.

Cenoz, J. and D. Gorter. 2011. 'A holistic approach to multilingual education: Introduction'. *Modern Language Journal* 95: 339–343.

Charalambous, P., C. Charalambous., and M. Zembylas. 2016. 'Troubling translanguaging: Language ideologies, superdiversity and interethnic conflict'. *Applied Linguistics Review* 7: 327–352.

Cook, V. 1999. 'Going beyond the native speaker in language teaching'. *TESOL Quarterly* 33 (2): 185–209

Council of Europe. (n.d.). *Policies for plurilingualism*. Council of Europe, Education and Language, Language Policy. Accessed 14 May 2021. http://www.coe.int/t/dg4/linguistic

Creese, A. and A. Blackledge. 2010. 'Translanguaging in the bilingual classroom: A pedagogy for learning and teaching'. *Modern Language Journal* 94: 103–115.

Doiz, A. and D. Lasagabaster. 2017. 'Teachers' beliefs about translanguaging practices'. In C. M. Mazak and K. S. Carroll (eds.), *Translanguaging in higher education: Beyond monolingual ideologies*. Bristol, UK: Multilingual Matters. 157–176.

Donato, R. 1994. 'Collective scaffolding in second language learning'. In J. P. Lantolf and G. Appel (eds.), *Vygotskian approaches to second language research*. Norwood, NJ: Ablex. 33–56.

Duarte, J. 2019. 'Translanguaging in mainstream education: A sociocultural approach'. *International Journal of Bilingual Education and Bilingualism* 22 (2): 1–15.

Ellis, E. M. 2008. 'Defining and investigating monolingualism'. *Sociolinguistic Studies* 2 (3): 311–330.

Fairclough, N. 1992. *Discourse and social change*. Cambridge: Polity Press.

García, O. 2009. *Bilingual education in the 21st century: A global perspective*. Malden, MA: Wiley-Blackwell.

García, O., N. Flores., and H. H. Woodley. 2012. 'Transgressing monolingualism and bilingual dualities: Translanguaging pedagogies'. In A. Yiakoumetti (ed.), *Harnessing linguistic variation to improve education*. Bern, Switzerland: Peter Lang. pp. 45–75.

García, O. and C. Leiva. 2014. 'Theorizing and enacting translanguaging for social justice'. In A. Blackledge and A. Creese (eds.), *Heteroglossia as practice and pedagogy*. New York, NY: Springer. 199–216.

García, O. and W Li. 2014. *Translanguaging: Language, bilingualism and education*. Basingstoke: Palgrave Macmillan.

Grosjean, F. 1985. The bilingual as a competent but specific speaker-hearer. *Journal of Multilingual and Multicultural Development* 6 (6): 467–477.

Gynne, A. and S. Bagga-Gupta. 2015. 'Languaging in the twenty-first century: Exploring varieties and modalities in literacies inside and outside learning spaces'. *Language and Education* 29: 509–526.

Ho, W. Y. J. and W. Li. 2019. 'Mobilising learning: A translanguaging view'. *Chinese Semiotic Studies* 15 (4): 533–559.

Hornberger, N. H. and H. Link. 2012. 'Translanguaging in today's classrooms: A biliteracy lens'. *Theory into Practice* 51: 239–247.

Iedema, R. 2003. 'Multimodality, resemiotization extending the analysis of discourse as multi-semiotic practice'. *Visual Communication* 2: 29–57.

Jaspers, J. 2018. 'The transformative limits of translanguaging'. *Language and Communication* 58: 1–10.

Jewitt, C. 2009. 'An introduction to multimodality'. In C. Jewitt (ed.), *The Routledge handbook of multimodal analysis*. London: Routledge. 14–27.

Kress, G. 2015. 'Semiotic work: Applied linguistics and a social semiotic account of Multimodality'. *AILA Review* 28: 49–71.

Lantolf, J. P. and A. Aljaafreh. 1996. 'Second language learning in the zone of proximal development: A revolutionary experience'. *International Journal of Educational Research* 23: 619–632.

Lefebvre, H. 1991. *The production of space*. Oxford: Blackwell.

Lewis, G., B. Jones, and C. Baker. 2012. 'Translanguaging: Developing its conceptualisation and contextualization'. *Educational Research and Evaluation* 18: 655–670.

Li, W. 2011. 'Moment analysis and translanguaging space: Discursive construction of identities by multilingual Chinese youth in Britain'. *Journal of Pragmatics* 43: 1222–1235.

Li, W. 2014. 'Translanguaging knowledge and identity in complementary classrooms for multilingual minority ethnic children'. *Classroom Discourse* 5: 158–175.

Li, W. 2018. 'Translanguaging as a practical theory of language'. *Applied Linguistics* 39: 9–30.

Li, W. 2020. 'Multilingual English users' linguistic innovation'. *World Englishes* 39: 236–248.

Li, W. and J. W. Y. Ho. 2018. 'Language learning sans frontiers: A translanguaging view'. *Annual Review of Applied Linguistics* 38: 33–59.

Li, W. and H. Zhu. 2013. 'Translanguaging identities: Creating transnational space through flexible multilingual practices amongst Chinese university students in the UK'. *Applied Linguistics* 34 (5): 516–535.

Licona, P. 2015. *Translanguaging in a middle school science classroom: Constructing scientific arguments in English and Spanish*. PhD thesis. The Pennsylvania State University.

Lin, A. M. Y. and P. He 2017. 'Translanguaging as dynamic activity flows in CLIL classrooms'. *Journal of Language, Identity and Education* 16: 228–244.

Lin, A. M. Y. and Y. Wu. 2015. '"May I speak Cantonese?" – Co-constructing a scientific proof in an EFL junior secondary science classroom'. *International Journal of Bilingual Education and Bilingualism* 18: 289–305.

Makalela, L. 2015. 'Moving out of linguistic boxes: the effects of translanguaging strategies for multilingual classrooms'. *Language and Education* 29: 200–217.

Matsumoto, Y. and A. Dobs. 2017. 'Pedagogical gestures as interactional resources for teaching and learning tense and aspect in the ESL grammar classroom'. *Language Learning* 67 (1): 7–42.

Mazak, C. and C. Herbas-Donoso. 2015. 'Translanguaging practices at a bilingual university: A case study of a science classroom'. *International Journal of Bilingual Education and Bilingualism*. 18: 698–714.

McCarthy, M. 1991. *Discourse analysis for language teachers*. Cambridge: Cambridge University Press.

Nikula, T. and P. Moore. 2019. 'Exploring translanguaging in CLIL'. *International Journal of Bilingual Education and Bilingualism* 22 (2): 237–249.

Norris, S. 2004. *Analyzing multimodal interaction: A methodological framework*. London: Routledge.

Otheguy, R., O. García, and W. Reid. 2015. 'Clarifying translanguaging and deconstructing named languages: A perspective from linguistics'. *Applied Linguistics Review* 6 (3): 281–307.

Palmer, D., R. A. Martínez, S. G. Matteus., and K. Henderson. 2014. 'Reframing the debate on language separation: Toward a vision for translanguaging pedagogies in the dual language classroom'. *Modern Language Journal* 98: 757–772.

Potter, J. 1996. Discourse analysis and constructionist approaches: Theoretical background. In J. T. E. Richards (ed.), *Handbook of qualitative research methods for psychology and the social sciences*. Leicester: British Psychological Society. 125–140.

Probyn, M. 2019. 'Pedagogical translanguaging and the construction of science knowledge in a multilingual South African classroom: Challenging monoglossic/post-colonial orthodoxies'. *Classroom Discourse* 10 (3–4): 216–236.

Psathas, G. 1995. *Conversation analysis: The study of talk-in-interaction*. Thousand Oaks, CA: Sage.

Rampton, B. 2006. *Language in late modernity: Interaction in an urban school*. Cambridge: Cambridge University Press.

Rothman, J. 2008. 'Linguistic epistemology and the notion of monolingualism'. *Sociolinguistic Studies* 2 (3): 441–458.

Sah, P. and G. Li. 2022. 'Translanguaging or unequal languaging? Unfolding the plurilingual discourse of English medium instruction (EMI) in Nepal's public schools'. *International Journal of Bilingual Education and Bilingualism* 25 (6): 2075–2094.

Seedhouse, P. 2004. *The interactional architecture of the language classroom: A conversation analysis perspective*. London: Blackwell.

Selinker, L. 1972. 'Interlanguage'. *International Review of Applied Linguistics* 10: 209–231.

Selinker, L. 1974. 'An error in error analysis'. *Language Learning* 8 (24): 23–28.

Smotrova, T. and J. P. Lantolf. 2013. 'The function of gesture in lexically focused L2 instructional conversations'. *Modern Language Journal* 97 (2): 397–416.

Swain, M. 2006. 'Languaging, agency and collaboration in advanced second language proficiency'. In H. Byrnes (ed.). *Advanced language learning: The contribution of halliday and vygotsky*. London: Continuum. 95–108.

Tai, K. W. H. 2022a. 'Translanguaging as inclusive pedagogical practices in English medium instruction science and mathematics classrooms for linguistically and culturally diverse students'. *Research in Science Education* 52: 975–1012.

Tai, K. W. H. 2022b. 'A translanguaging perspective on teacher contingency in Hong Kong English medium instruction history classrooms'. *Applied Linguistics*. Epub ahead of print. https://doi.org/10.1093/applin/amac039

Tai, K. W. H. 2023a. 'Cross-curricular connection in an Hong Kong English medium instruction western history classroom: A translanguaging view'. *Language and Education*. Epub ahead of print. https://doi.org/10.1080/095 00782.2023.2174379

Tai, K. W. H. 2023b. 'Managing classroom misbehaviours in the Hong Kong English medium instruction secondary classrooms: A translanguaging perspective'. *System* 113: 1–35.
Tai, K. W. H. and A. Brandt. 2018. 'Creating an imaginary context: Teacher's use of embodied enactments in addressing learner's initiatives in a beginner-level adult ESOL classroom'. *Classroom Discourse* 9 (3): 244–266.
Tai, K. W. H. and N. Khabbazbashi. 2019a. 'The mediation and organisation of gestures in vocabulary instructions: A microgenetic analysis of interactions in a beginning-level adult ESOL classroom'. *Language and Education* 33 (5): 445–468.
Tai, K. W. H. and N. Khabbazbashi. 2019b. 'Vocabulary explanations in beginning-level adult ESOL classroom interactions: A conversation analysis perspective'. *Linguistics and Education* 52: 61–77.
Tai, K. W. H. and W. Li. 2020. 'Bringing the outside in: Connecting students' out-of-school knowledge and experience through translanguaging in Hong Kong English medium instruction mathematics classes'. *System* 95: 1–32.
Tai, K. W. H. and W. Li. 2021a. 'The affordances of iPad for constructing a technology-mediated space in Hong Kong English medium instruction secondary classrooms: A translanguaging view'. *Language Teaching Research*. Epub ahead of Print. https://doi.org/10.1177/13621688211027851
Tai, K. W. H. and W. Li. 2021b. 'Co-learning in Hong Kong English medium instruction mathematics secondary classrooms: A translanguaging perspective'. *Language and Education* 35 (3): 241–267.
Tai, K. W. H. and W. Li. 2021c. 'Constructing playful talk through translanguaging in the English medium instruction mathematics classrooms'. *Applied Linguistics* 42 (4): 607–640.
Tai, K. W. H. and W. Li. 2023. 'Embodied enactment of a hypothetical scenario in an English medium instruction secondary mathematics classroom: A translanguaging approach'. *Language Teaching Research*. Epub ahead of print. https://doi.org/10.1177/13621688231152858
Tai, K. W. H. and B. L. M. Poon. 2016. 'A conversation analysis of teacher's feedback and students' uptake in an intermediate English as a second language classroom at INTO Newcastle University'. *Annual Review of Education, Communication and Language Sciences (ARECLS)* 13: 15–43.
Tai, K. W. H. and C. Y. Wong. 2022. 'Empowering students through the construction of a translanguaging space in an English as a first language classroom'. *Applied Linguistics*. Epub ahead of print. https://doi.org/10.1093/applin/amac069
Thibault, P. J. 2011. 'First-order languaging dynamics and second-order language: The distributed language view'. *Ecological Psychology* 23: 210–245.
Thibault, P. J. 2017. 'The reflexivity of human languaging and Nigel Love's two orders of language'. *Language Sciences* 61: 74–85.
Vygotsky, L. S. 1978. *Mind in society: The development of higher psychological processes*. Cambridge, MA: Harvard University Press.
Wang, D. 2019. *Multilingualism and translanguaging in chinese language classrooms*. Cham, Switzerland: Palgrave Macmillan.

Wantanabe, Y. 2004. *Collaborative dialogue between ESL learners of different proficiency levels: Linguistic and affective outcomes.* M.A. Thesis, University of Toronto.

Williams, C. 1994. *An evaluation of teaching and learning methods in the context of bilingual secondary education.* PhD thesis, University of Wales, Bangor.

Williams, C. 2002. *A study of language immersion at 11–16 years of age.* Bangor, UK: School of Education.

Woodley, H. H. 2016. 'Balancing windows and mirrors: Translanguaging in a linguistically diverse classroom'. In T. Kleyn and O. García (eds.), *Translanguaging with multilingual students: Learning from classroom moments.* New York: Taylor and Francis. 83–100.

Zhu, H., W. Li, and A. Lyons. 2017. 'Polish shop(ping) as translanguaging space'. *Social Semiotics* 27: 411–433.

3 Multimodal Conversation Analysis for Investigating the Process of Classroom Translanguaging

3.1 Multimodal Conversation Analysis

MCA, with its roots in ethnomethodology and sociology, 'focuses on how social order is co-constructed by the members of a social group' (Brouwer and Wagner, 2004: 30) through fine-grained analysis of the social interaction. It takes an emic/participant-relevant approach (Markee and Kasper, 2004) in order to explicate the detailed process of how social actions, such as learning, are co-organised and achieved through talk-in-interaction. MCA allows researchers to analyse naturally occurring interactions, and every minute detail 'is considered relevant in uncovering participant orientations toward the interaction' (Waring, 2008: 580). The analytic stance of MCA requires researchers not to pre-theorise the relevance and importance of language-in-use, which entails semiotic resources including eye gaze and gestures. The analytical focus must be on sequences instead of on isolated turns or utterances (Hutchby and Wooffitt, 1998). A key feature of MCA is that it views interaction as structurally organised. Heritage (1995: 396) points out the following: 'social interaction is informed by institutionalized structural organizations of practices to which participants are normatively oriented'. This suggests that social interaction is patterned, that there should be an interactional pattern known among interlocutors, and that they should orient to such order during the conversations.

As a result of 'empirically based accounts of the observable conversational behaviours of participants' (Markee, 2005: 355), MCA research has discovered several formal features of talk including turn-taking, adjacency pair, repair, and preferred and dispreferred organisations (ten Have, 2007). These formal interactional features offer a useful starting point for researchers when analysing interactions in different social contexts. However, as Richards (2006: 13) argues, 'the emphasis in the analysis [...] is not on how interactants obey the relevant rules, but on how they jointly construct the conversation and their shared understanding of what is happening in it'. MCA analysts need to pay attention to how talk unfolds and not investigate utterances in isolation. Therefore, when examining interaction on a turn-by-turn basis, the spoken interaction has to be carefully transcribed, including detailed information regarding pausing, pitch, or pace, with 'a ferocious attention to detail that not all researchers can muster' (Richards, 2003: 28). This is because the construction of social interaction offers as much information regarding meaning and context as its content.

MCA is also considered as a useful research method for studying how language policies are implemented in actual practices. Spolsky (2004) suggests that studying the effectiveness of language policies involves analysing actual language use since speakers use interactional norms to make sense of their language choice, in terms of knowing what language(s) should be used or not in a particular social context. Bonacina-Pugh (2012) argues that Conversation Analysis (CA) allows analysts to analyse talk-in-interaction and identify the set of interactional norms that speakers orient to in social interaction. From a CA perspective, speakers employ these interactional norms to interpret each other's language use, that is, as 'a point of reference or action template for interpretation' (Seedhouse, 2004: 10). Therefore, these interactional norms are not prescriptive or 'rules', but they are the speaker's implicit understanding of what should be done. In this sense, such an understanding informs the speakers' interpretation and production of utterances in social action. Bonacina-Pugh (2020) illustrates how CA can be deployed to reveal practiced language policies in an induction classroom for newly arrived immigrant children in France, where French is the medium of instruction. The findings demonstrate that there are moments when the teacher and students orient towards the declared and perceived language policies of the French educational system. Bonacina-Pugh also demonstrates that the classroom participants orient towards a practiced language policy (Bonacina-Pugh, 2012) which legitimates them for using multiple languages other than French. This sense of legitimacy is negotiated at the local level of classroom interaction, and it is repeatedly followed by other classroom participants.

Moreover, Spolsky and Shohamy (2000) argue that a way to study a language policy within language use is to investigate its 'non-observance' (p. 29). This refers to the observed patterns where speakers do not follow what is typically done. These can potentially justify the implicit and deducible rules that 'are not always observable, but [...] their non-observance is noticeable, in the way that a car driving faster than the speed limit is noticeable but does not disprove the existence of a law controlling speed' (p. 29). The examination of 'non-observance' is related to deviant case analysis which is a useful CA tool for analysts to examine cases that are dissimilar from the previously examined interactional phenomenon (Heritage, 1984). Using CA as the methodological approach allows analysts to identify deviant cases by paying attention to participants' orientation. As Bonacina-Pugh (2012) argues, by examining the participant's orientation to deviant cases, this enables CA analysts to deduce what a normative case will be. In other words, studying deviant cases can illuminate what interactional norm speakers are orienting to in interaction which can shed light on whether a language(s) is considered legitimate or not and when.

Bonacina-Pugh (2012, 2020) has illustrated the potential of using CA as an efficient methodological tool for examining the enactment of language policies in multilingual classrooms. To date, a few researchers in the field of second language acquisition (e.g., Lin and Wu, 2015; Jakonen et al., 2018) have adapted MCA as a method to explore translanguaging practices in multilingual classroom settings. The findings of the studies (e.g., Jakonen et al., 2018) illustrate that MCA is effective in explicating the detailed process of how translanguaging practices are jointly constructed between teachers and students in EMI classrooms, although classroom participants are expected to use the target language (i.e., English) throughout the lessons under the monolingual policy. Many linguistic ethnographers utilise MCA as the linguistic framework of their studies (e.g., Copland, 2011; Rock, 2017; Matsumoto, 2018) due to its focus on linguistic form in interaction when integrated with ethnographic information. This allows for the data to be triangulated and for multiple interpretations of a particular social action. When reporting findings, linguistic ethnographers can offer linguistic evidence for the arguments that they make, which addresses the criticism of ethnographic work that it is heavily reliant on the researcher's own interpretation of the research setting. MCA also offers a set of formal features for how speakers behave in interactions, and any identified atypical interactional features can bear further investigation.

3.2 Basic Principles of Conversation Analysis

According to Seedhouse (2004: 166–167), the basic principles of CA are as follows:

1. 'There is order at all points in interaction: Talk in interaction is systematically organised, deeply ordered and methodic.
2. Contributions to interaction are context-shaped and context-renewing: Contributions to interaction cannot be adequately understood excerpt by reference to the sequential environment in which they occur and in which the participants design them to occur. They also form part of the sequential environment in which a next contribution will occur.
3. No order of detail can be dismissed a priori as disorderly, accidental, or irrelevant (Heritage, 1984: 241): CA has a detailed transcription system, and a highly empirical orientation.
4. Analysis is bottom-up and data-driven: The data should not be approached with any prior theoretical assumptions, regarding, for example, power, gender, or race; unless there is evidence in the details of the interaction that the interactants themselves are orienting to it.'

The first point suggests that there is 'order at all points' (Sacks, 1984: 22) in spoken interaction. In other words, MCA's essential finding is the organised system of turn-taking in conversation. It accounts for the sequential structure of talk-in-interaction in terms of real-time orientations to the preferential practices that underlie, for participants and consequently also for MCA analysts, the conversational behaviours of turn-taking and repair in different speech exchange systems. MCA focuses on particular subsets of recurring phenomena and systematises the findings (Psathas, 1995). Nevertheless, it is vital to note that the goal of using MCA to analyse translanguaging should not be identifying recurring patterns. As Li (2018) argues, adopting a translanguaging perspective requires analysts to focus on the spontaneity and transient nature of social interaction. By doing so, the analysts need to move beyond looking for patterns with regularity. In other words, MCA analysts can turn the analytical focus on capturing how speakers make good use of the affordances of various resources creatively to transcend the standards of the named languages and the sociocultural norms (Li, 2018; Tai and Li, 2020, 2021a, 2021b, 2021c, 2023). This will be further explained in Section 3.5.

The second point refers to the idea that classroom interactions are context shaped and context renewing. Teachers and students will make sense of each other's turns, and their next contribution to the interaction depends on their understanding of each other's contributions. For example, when producing an action, teachers and students will relate the action to a previous action. The contextualised location shapes their actions with the sequential environment, and hence classroom interaction is context shaped. On the other hand, when the classroom participant produces an action, the participant will make relevant his or her subsequent contribution, which should be performed by other participants. As such, the participant's action constructs a new context—that is, context shaping.

The third point relates to the need for MCA analysts to capture all details of talk and multimodal phenomena in the transcripts. By providing as much information as possible from the recordings, this allows analysts to conduct fine-grained and thorough analysis of the social interactions. Finally, the MCA analysis has to be data-driven, and through adopting an emic perspective, analysts should not bring in prior assumptions or theories to affect the interpretations of the analysis. MCA analysts aim to understand the orientations which the participants display to one another through their observable actions within the social interaction. Hence, no prior theories or assumption should be made unless the participants make them relevant in the interaction. MCA analysts tend to draw on transcription conventions developed by Jefferson (2004) and Mondada (2018) in order to offer a detailed record of the social interaction (see Appendix for the detailed descriptions of the transcription conventions).

3.3 Key Interactional Features in Social Interactions

In Section 3.3, I have briefly introduced the important notions in terms of interactional organisation, which includes turn-taking, adjacency pairs, and repair. In this section, I am going to explain these notions in greater detail in order to demonstrate how these interactional structures assist readers and analysts to understand the nature of social interactions.

3.3.1 Adjacency Pairs

Adjacency pairs refer to the paired utterances, that is, the first pair part (FPP) and the second pair part (SPP), that are produced by different speakers and are conditionally relevant (Schegloff and Sacks, 1973). In other words, the FPP should be made relevant to the next action and completed by the SPP. Schegloff and Sacks (1973) identify four properties of adjacency pairs:

1   They happen adjacently to one another.
2   They are uttered by different participants.

3   They are ordered. That is, the production of an FPP (e.g., question) will be followed by an SPP (e.g., answer).
4   They are type-matched. In other words, a specific FPP makes a related SPP.

For example, a question occupies an FPP position while an answer occupies an SPP position. When an FPP is uttered, a type-matched SPP is typically expected. Nevertheless, if the SPP is not produced, its absence may still be considered as relevant and accountable. This is because the absence of a response may result in 'attention to issues of non-hearing, nonunderstanding, misunderstanding, or to a repetition of the first or a disruption in the continuity of the interaction, and so on' (Psathas, 1995, p. 21). Hence, identifying the adjacency pairs allow the MCA analysts to assess and understand the interlocutors' actions and interactional engagement (Seedhouse, 2004).

3.3.2 Turn-Taking

Turns are "the interactionally validated units of talk" (Ford and Thompson, 1996: 136). Turn-taking practices are made up of 'turn-construction units' (TCUs). This can be perceived as a single social action that is performed in a turn. TCUs can be defined at a linguistic level, such as through sentences, words, or clauses, and also at a level of non-verbal action, such as silence, laughter, or gestures. In other words, TCU is 'essentially a social concept rather than a linguistic one and cannot therefore be delimited in linguistic terms' (Seedhouse, 2004: 30). Moreover, Ford and Thompson (1996: 136) argue that 'the end of any such unit is a possible completion of a turn, and possible completions of turns are places at which potential next speakers appropriately start next turns'. That is, when a speaker has completed a meaningful utterance, there is a space where a transition to another speaker may occur. This space is known as the 'transition-relevance places' (TRP). A TRP can potentially lead to a transfer of speakership. Nevertheless, whether the transition of speakers can successfully be projected by a TCU depends on the participants' understanding of the local context.

3.3.3 Repair

Another important term that is key to MCA is repair. Repair is defined as 'the treatment of trouble occurring in interactive language use' (Seedhouse, 2004: 34). Trouble can be anything that the participants perceive as hindering their communication. This can have an impact on achieving mutual understanding between speakers during the social interactions. As Seedhouse (2004: 34) further suggests, repair is a 'vital mechanism for the maintenance of reciprocity of perspectives and intersubjectivity', which is a constant display of mutual understanding of each other's actions. There are four types of repair, which are characterised by 'the initiation of repair (marking something as a source of trouble), and the actual repair itself' (Hutchby and Wooffitt, 2008: 61):

- Self-initiated self-repair: Repair is both initiated and carried out by the speaker of the trouble source.
- Other-initiated self-repair: Repair is carried out by the speaker of the trouble source but initiated by the recipient.
- Self-initiated other-repair: The speaker of a trouble source may get the recipient to repair the trouble source.
- Other-initiated other-repair: The recipient of a trouble-source both initiates and carries out the repair.

It is vital for L2 teachers and students to understand how breakdowns in classroom interaction and miscommunication can be repaired. As van Lier (1988: 211) argues, 'we must bear in mind that certain types of activity naturally lead to certain types of repair, and therefore the issue of how to repair is closely related to the context of what is being done'. Kasper (1986: 39) compares the organisation of repair in language-focused and content-focused L2 lessons, and she concludes that:

> talking about repair in foreign language teaching as such is inconclusive: rather, preferences and dis-preferences for specific repair patterns depend on the configuration of relevant factors in the classroom context […] The teaching goal of the two phases turned out to be the decisive factor for the selection of repair patterns.

In other words, the organisation of repair varies since it depends on the pedagogical focus at that particular moment of the classroom interaction. Moreover, what considers trouble differs with the pedagogical goal, which means that what constitutes as repairable is different in each context (Seedhouse, 2004).

3.4 Data Analysis Procedures

3.4.1 Identifying Translanguaging Instances

The identification of translanguaging instances is critical for conducting MCA analysis. As I have mentioned in Chapter 2, I consider translanguaging as practices where participants draw on their multilingual and multimodal resources from their repertoires in a fluid and dynamic manner to construct meaning (Li, 2018) in the multilingual classroom setting. Through adopting translanguaging as an analytical perspective, this allows researchers to identify how teachers and students move between their full linguistic and semiotic repertoires when they interact in the lessons. Therefore, when analysing classroom video data, researchers will need to look for translanguaging instances which involve going beyond different linguistic structures and systems (i.e., not only different languages and dialects, but also styles, registers, and other variations in language use) and different modalities (e.g., switching between speaking and writing, or coordinating gestures, body movements, facial expressions, or visual images). The identifications of translanguaging instances in the data are relied on the analysis of the interaction itself.

In order to ensure that the MCA analysis is reliable and valid, the identified translanguaging practices need to be solidified by reiterative line-by-line analyses of the data to minimise the possibility of any subjective interpretations. Throughout the re-analysis process, we need to strive to maintain the 'radically emic perspective'. Moreover, it is recommended that researchers can invite other MCA researchers to review selected transcript segments and the corresponding videos in the sessions. Having other MCA analysts examining my data can bring a 'fresh' eye to the data and make sure that the analysis is not the researcher's own 'interpretation', but 'sharable and shared understandings which can [...] be analysed in procedural terms' (ten Have, 2007: 140).

3.4.2 Transcription of Classroom Interaction Data

When transcribing the classroom interaction data, researchers can use the transcription conventions developed by Jefferson (2004) and Mondada (2018) for providing a detailed record of the discourse (see Appendix for the transcription conventions). Transcriptions allow the readers to observe the complexity of the nature of talk. As Hutchby and Wooffitt (2008: 69) suggest, transcription of data is an important procedure at the core of MCA analysis:

> Transcription is a necessary initial step in enabling the analysis of recorded interaction in the way that CA requires. Secondly, the practice of transcription and production of transcript represent a distinctive stage in the process of data analysis itself.

Therefore, transcription is acknowledged as the orthographic representation of the data which becomes the basis of the MCA analysis. However, it is crucial to note that 'transcripts are not the data of CA, but rather a convenient way to capture and present the phenomena of interest in written form' (ten Have, 2007). It is possible that any transcription conducted by different researchers can be affected by their own theoretical approach to the data (Lapadat and Lindsay, 1999). The position that most MCA researchers hold is that a transcript should include as many details as possible since nothing is considered as irrelevant. Minute details, such as intonations, nonverbal resources, and length of silence, are needed as these details could inform researchers regarding 'how social actions are performed, how each turn is produced and treated by the participants' (ten Have, 2007: 89).

However, many MCA researchers transcribe the data to different levels of detail (Brandt, 2011). Each MCA analyst needs to decide how much detail they will transcribe. This is because MCA principles, to some extent, do not comply with real-life practicalities, and the transcription process can take many months. Therefore, it is recommended that researchers can first do a 'rough' transcription initially which involves the spoken utterances and some other notable features (e.g., gestures). Further details that are potentially relevant to the research topic are added after watching the video data multiple times. Multimodal aspects of the transcripts are also included in the transcript to explore the switch of communicative modes in the classrooms. For the purpose of my research, screenshots are integrated into the transcripts to enhance clarity for readers. A '+' sign is used to indicate the onset of nonverbal actions (Sert, 2017). A '#' sign is employed for the screenshots to indicate to the readers the exact locations of the figures in the transcripts. '*--->' is used to describe the action that is continued across subsequent lines, and '--->*' represents the end of the action (Mondada, 2018). In order to represent the multilingual talk, English translations are highlighted in italics and placed after the verbal features of talk on a separate line (see Appendix for more transcription conventions).

3.4.3 Data Analysis

MCA analysis of the video data first involves adhering to the principle of 'unmotivated' looking. This requires the researchers to ground the research focus based on the recordings of the interactions without referring to the external factors that are unacknowledged by the participants in order to develop an emic understanding of the classroom interaction. Although one may argue that all looking is motivated (e.g., Psathas, 1995), the idea is that a research study should look 'openly' without any particular interest of focus before conducting further exploratory analysis. Therefore, it is important for researchers to explore the video data with an open mind rather than assuming that translanguaging practices will definitely emerge in the video data. When identifying translanguaging practices, collections of similar occurrences are built up and differences and similarities between cases are identified in order to reveal different aspects or features of translanguaging practices (Sidnell, 2010).

Line-by-line analysis is conducted to examine how talk is sequentially organised on a turn-by-turn basis, relating each utterance to what was said before and what comes after. Prior MCA studies have discovered a number of interactional features of talk, including turn-taking, pausing, repair, adjacency pair, and multimodality (Waring, 2008; Brandt, 2011; Sert, 2017). These interactional features provide a useful starting point when studying how translanguaging is sequentially organised. However, as Richards (2006: 13) argues, 'the emphasis in the analysis […] is not on how interactants obey the relevant rules, but on how they jointly construct the conversation and their shared understanding of what is happening in it'. Therefore, MCA researchers need to pay attention to how talk unfolds and not examine participants' utterances in isolation from the contextual environment. That is, the meaning of the talk is shaped and displayed in the environment in which it occurs (Kasper, 2009).

3.5 Research Studies on Using CA to Investigate Translanguaging in Multilingual Classrooms

To date, a few researchers in the field of applied linguistics (e.g., Lin and Wu, 2015; Jakonen et al., 2018) have adapted CA as a method to explore translanguaging practices in multilingual classroom settings. For instance, Lin and Wu's (2015) study is one of the few studies, to the best of my knowledge, that employs CA to investigate how learners use translanguaging to actively construct meaning and display understanding in a year 8 HK EMI science classroom. Based on the analysis of a five-minute classroom interaction, the findings indicate that the teacher mostly follows the rigid initiation–response–feedback schema and does not attempt to activate her learners' L1, Cantonese, to scaffold their access to the science discourse in English. However, when the teacher grants permission to a low-proficiency learner to answer the

MCA for Investigating the Process of Classroom Translanguaging 43

teacher's response in Cantonese, it provides an opportunity for the learner to initiate an extended sequence in Cantonese which contradicts with her struggling effort in articulating her previous response in English. This is revealed in the following extract from the study:

In this extract, the science teacher is inviting students to think about the phenomenon of compressed air. When the teacher continues to initiate follow-up questions to engage to think about how air has mass (line 22), Alice enunciates a request to allow her to speak in Cantonese: 'may I speak Cantonese?' (line 23). Here, it is noticeable that Alice is orienting towards the institutional language policy, which only allows English to be used in EMI lessons. The teacher grants permission to Alice to employ Cantonese in line 25, which encourages Alice to produce an extended utterance in Cantonese in line 26. Noticeably, Alice's long response involves examples of translanguaging. She first refers to the oxygen tanks as '空氣 (air)' rather than '氧氣筒 (oxygen tank)'.

14	Alex (boy at the front):	Use to (.) Try to (.) =
15	Ray (boy at the back):	=°Compress° *[seems not heard by Alex at the front]*
16	T:	=Compress *[gesturing the action of compress]*
17	Alex (boy at the front):	=compress it. And then if you can't compress it out, because you use your finger to cover the mouth. And then (.) it takes up space.
18	T:	Right. One very good evidence, say if I use a syringe = *[T draws on the blackboard as she speaks]*
19	T:	= and I block it with my finger *[T draws on the blackboard a big andcute hand beside the syringe. Ss laugh, probably at her funny drawing. See Figure 1.].* And then I compress the syringe. You will find that finallyyou can't compress it anymore. In other words, you can see the space cannot be further compressed because of the air inside. Or another example. When you blow a balloon = *[T draws on the blackboard as she speaks]*
20	T:	= you can see the balloon getting bigger. What do you blow into the balloon?
21	Ss:	Air.
22	T:	If it doesn't take up space, how can the balloon get bigger? So you can see that air takes up space. How can I prove that air has mass? How can I prove that? (.) You can't even see it, feel it. How can you prove that air has mass?
23	Alice (girl at the front):	Eh (5) You (.) you (.) you (.) May I speak Cantonese?
24	Alex (boy at the front):	Yes, I can use Cantonese.
25	T:	Yes, go ahead.
26	Alice (girl at the front):	好似果 D 潛水員帶果 D, 將果D 空氣壓縮左嘎嘛'但系重左嘎嘛'本來毋野'但壓縮左之後就重左嘎嘛 (trans. Like what the diver carries. The air is compressed, but it is heavier. Initially, here there is nothing, but it is heavier after compression)
27	T:	You are talk (.) OK, how do I know it is heavier? What do you use to measure?

Figure 3.1 Lin and Wu, 2015: 304–305.

This shows that Alice does not know the specific vocabulary of oxygen tank in Cantonese. However, Alice utilises the Cantonese word '壓縮 (compress)', which is a formal Cantonese word, rather than an everyday Cantonese word, to explain how a diver is carrying a tank of compressed air. It is evidenced that Alice picks up the scientific word 'compress' from the interaction (lines 15–17, 19) and searches for the Cantonese equivalent for 'compress'. The authors argue that creating a space for students to translanguage by drawing on their familiar linguistic resources, both everyday and academic wordings, is effective in assisting with their learning of the scientific knowledge.

Building on Lin and Wu's (2015) study, Jakonen et al. (2018) employ CA to analyse how a student's translanguaging practices subvert the English-only norm in a junior secondary CLIL history classroom in Finland and is treated as 'language mixing' by other peers. The analysis illustrates that the student's translanguaging practices involve deploying a wide range of linguistic resources, through combining lexical items and grammar of English and Finnish and uttering English words with a stereotypical Finnish accent, to create a linguistic form which is highly creative and hybrid. This is illuminated in the following extract adapted from the study:

This extract demonstrates how the students' orientations of the medium of instruction differ from each other. In the extract, Sakari is narrating a story about his experience in the morning. His narrative consists of using a range of linguistic resources, which is being judged by his peers as 'bad English'. For example, in line 33, Sakari introduces the story by saying that he throws coffee on the table cloth. Particularly, Sakari makes use of a Swedish verb 'drycka (to drink)' and Finnish alongside English in constructing the turn. Such a telling is marked as funny, as signalled by Inka's comment in line 35 and Sakina's own laughter in line 36, because spilling a cup of coffee is being described as an act of throwing. Moreover, Sakari also mixes prepositions and definite articles of English in line 36, such as 'in' and 'a', with Finnish vocabulary to convey the progressivity of the story. As shown, Sakari is translanguaging as he utilises a range of linguistic resources, including different lexical items (e.g., in line 33) but also the grammatical features of English and Finnish to create the story for the audience. Nevertheless, there are two girls, Inka and Susanna, who use English to display an orientation to the English-only language policy. When the girls are suggesting what Sakari can do to avoid embarrassment, the girls engage in a vocabulary search in English (lines 59–61) in order to maintain English as the medium of interaction (Bonacina-Pugh and Gafaranga, 2011). Hence, the authors suggest that the CA

(Finnish = bold, Swedish = bold and italics)

```
31          (1.5)
32   Ink    oikeesti [(xx)    ]
            'really (xx)'
33   Sak             [jag hh,] (0.5)  dr[ycka  ]coffee, (.) aamulla and=
                      'I                drink  coffee      in the morning and'
34   Ink                                  [<you,>]
35          =you [a::re (.) >bad<]
36   Sak         [heittää it      ] on the pöytäl(h)i(h)in(h)a hhh hehe
                  'to throw'              'table cloth'
37          (0.9)
38   Sus    why
39   Sak    I was (.) on (.) computer and then I (.) do like, (0.4)
40          >I don't know< and [(then-)]
41   Sus                       [ com↑pu]ter morning? (([ kǫm'puːtːɛr 'mɔrnɪŋ]))
42          (0.4)
43   Sak    ye::s hhh
44          (0.8)
45   Ink    >määki oli<
            'I was too'
46          (0.6)
47   Ink    [I was] too.
48   Sak    [when,]
49          (0.6)
50   Sak    I was hh [(.) drinking coffee (0.4) I put the hh]
51   Sus             [I only listen (.) to music=           ]
52          =in computer morning=
53   Sak    =and then the hh (0.3) it was like white (.) the liina
                                                             'cloth'
54          and there's, (.) kauheet (.) läikät and my hh (0.5)
                              horrible-PL stain-PL
            'and there are horrible stains and my'
55          mom was in töissä I don't k(h)n(h)ow what to do, (0.4)
                         work-PL-INE
            'mom was at work I don't know what to do'
56          I (.) leave it (.) there
57   Ink    hhhh [he he he he he he .hh .hh
58   Sus         [hh he he he he .hh .hh
59   Ink    you should have (0.6) put it to::: straight away to the::
60          (0.7)
61   Sus    laundry
62          (1.1) ((INKA NODS))
63   Ink    eiko (.) >pyykki<koneesee
            'no I mean in the washing machine'
64          (0.8)
65   Sak    ye:s but (.) I don't know how to put it on
```

Figure 3.2 Jakonen et al., 2018: 38.

analysis illustrates the role of sequential contexts in establishing the meaning of translanguaging to participants since these sequential contexts can illuminate the locally upheld norms around linguistic choices.

As shown, the findings of the studies (e.g., Lin and Wu, 2015; Jakonen et al., 2018) have illustrated that CA is effective in explicating the detailed process of how translanguaging practices are jointly constructed between teachers and students in EMI classrooms although classroom participants are expected to use the target language (i.e., English) throughout the lessons under the monolingual policy. CA also offers a set of formal features for how speakers behave in interactions, and any identified atypical interactional features can bear further investigation. Nevertheless, there is still limited research conducting a fine-grained analysis to study the nature of translanguaging in multilingual classrooms. Particularly, most of these studies (e.g., Lin and Lo, 2017; Jakonen et al., 2018; Poza, 2018; Sah and Li, 2022; Nikula and Moore, 2019) only conceptualise translanguaging as a practice which indicates the movement among linguistic repertoires. A small body of research on translanguaging in multilingual classrooms (e.g., Lin and He, 2017; Canagarajah, 2018; Moore and Vallejo, 2018; Wu and Lin, 2019) is able to demonstrate translanguaging at work in different modalities through multimodal transcriptions. These studies clearly demonstrate the usefulness of adopting a multimodal view to describe and analyse the complexity of participants' translanguaging practices. To my own understanding, studies by Tai and colleagues (Tai and Li, 2020, 2021a, 2021b, 2021c, 2023; Tai, 2022a, 2022b, 2023a, 2023b; Tai and Wong, 2022) are the first kind of studies that adopt MCA to conduct fine-grained analysis to analyse how teachers and students employ different multilingual, multimodal, multisensory, and multisemiotic resources available to them to design their actions and facilitate the meaning-making processes. These studies will be discussed in greater detail in Chapter 5 in order to explicate the usefulness of using MCA to understand how translanguaging practices are constructed in real-time classroom interactions.

3.6 Limitations in Using MCA Only in Investigating Classroom Translanguaging

In this section, I will explicate some of the criticism against MCA as a methodology for studying translanguaging practices in classroom interactions.

First, it has been argued that MCA insists on revealing the details of talk in order to document the observable resources that speakers employ in constructing their actions in interactions (Schegloff, 1987). Such a perspective of context is often argued as being too narrow (e.g., Waring and Hruska, 2011; Waring et al., 2012; Matsumoto, 2018). For example, MCA analysis cannot allow researchers to explore how factors such as power, political issues, gender, and ethnicity shape the nature of the social interactions. In other words, MCA cannot reveal how participants bring various dimensions of personal history, ideologies, beliefs, and so on to create the translanguaging spaces in EMI classrooms (Li, 2011). However, these sociocultural factors may not emerge from the MCA analysis directly, but they can be explored through using interviews and/or ethnographic approach. Hence, using ethnographic data gained through interviews and fieldnotes potentially allow researchers to gather additional contextual information to inform the interpretations of my MCA analysis. (Copland, 2011; Matsumoto, 2018). This argument will be further explained in Chapter 5.

Second, MCA has been criticised as being obsessed with the mechanism of social interactions and the 'clacking of turns' (Moerman, 1988: xi). An extreme version of such a criticism has accused MCA research as 'trivial' (see ten Have, 1990). Nevertheless, this would appear to be a matter of opinion. Although some scholars may perceive MCA as 'unsociological' (Zimmerman and Boden, 1991: 19), some other scholars also question 'what could be more sociological than the constitution of social action, and its implementation in interaction?' (Schegloff, 1988: 99).

3.7 Summary

In this chapter, I have given a detailed overview of the MCA as a methodology for analysing classroom interaction data. I also introduce the transcriptions and data analysis procedures and provide data extracts from existing studies to demonstrate how translanguaging can be analysed by using MCA. Additionally, some criticisms and limitations of MCA for understanding translanguaging practices are described. Despite these limitations, it is argued that MCA is an appropriate methodology for studying how translanguaging is employed by classroom participants during the lessons. Nevertheless, I also argue that it is important to combine other methodological approaches with MCA to interpretively analyse the translanguaging practices because a flexible framework is needed in order to review the complexities of translanguaging practices in classroom talk.

The next chapter presents IPA as the methodological framework in order to understand why translanguaging is constructed at that moment of the classroom interaction.

References

Bonacina-Pugh, F. 2012. 'Researching 'practiced language policies': Insights from conversation analysis'. *Language Policy* 11 (3): 213–234.
Bonacina-Pugh, F. 2020. 'Legitimizing multilingual practices in the classroom: The role of the 'practiced language policy''. *International Journal of Bilingual Education and Bilingualism* 23 (4): 434–448.
Bonacina-Pugh, F. and J. Gafaranga. 2011. "Medium of instruction' versus 'medium of classroom interaction': Language choice in a French

complementary school classroom in Scotland'. *International Journal of Bilingual Education and Bilingualism* 14 (3): 319–334.

Brandt, A. 2011. *The maintenance of mutual understanding in online second language talk*. PhD thesis. Newcastle University, UK.

Brouwer, C. E. and J. Wagner. 2004. 'Developmental issues in second language conversation'. *Journal of Applied Linguistics* 1 (1): 29–47.

Canagarajah, A. S. 2018. 'Translingual practice as spatial repertoires: Expanding the paradigm beyond structuralist orientations'. *Applied Linguistics* 39 (1): 31–54.

Copland, F. 2011. 'Negotiating face in feedback conferences: A linguistic ethnographic analysis'. *Journal of Pragmatics* 43: 3832–3843.

Ford, C. E. and S. A. Thompson 1996. 'Interactional units in conversation: Syntactic, intonational, and pragmatic resource for the management of turns'. In E. Ochs., E. A. Schegloff and S. A. Thompson (eds.), *Interaction and grammar*. Cambridge: Cambridge University Press. 134–184.

Heritage, J. 1984. *Garfinkel and ethnomethodology*. Cambridge: Polity Press.

Heritage, J. 1995. 'Conversation analysis: Methodological aspects'. In U. M. Quasthoff (ed.), *Aspects of oral communication*. Berlin/New York: Walter de Gruyter. 391–418.

Hutchby, I. and R. Wooffitt. 1998. *Conversation analysis: Principles, practices and applications*. Malden, MA: Blackwell.

Hutchby, I. and R. Wooffitt. 2008. *Conversation analysis* (2nd ed.). Cambridge: Polity Press.

Jakonen, T., T. P. Szabó, and P. Laihonen. 2018. 'Translanguaging as playful subversion of a monolingual norm in the classroom'. In G. Mazzaferro (ed.), *Translanguaging in everyday practice*. Singapore: Springer. 31–48.

Jefferson, G. 2004. 'Glossary of transcript symbols with an introduction'. In G. Lerner (ed.), *Conversation analysis: Studies from the first generation*. Philadelphia: John Benjamins. 14–31.

Kasper, G. 1986. 'A stands for acquisition: A response to Firth and Wagner'. *Modern Language Journal* 81: 307–312.

Kasper, G. 2009. 'Locating cognition in second language interaction and learning: Inside the skull or in public view?' *International Review of Applied Linguistics* 47: 11–36.

Lapadat, J. C. and A. C. Lindsay. 1999. 'Transcription in research and practice: From standardization of technique to interpretive positionings'. *Qualitative Inquiry* 5 (1): 64–86.

Li, W. 2011. 'Moment analysis and translanguaging space: Discursive construction of identities by multilingual Chinese youth in Britain'. *Journal of Pragmatics* 43: 1222–1235.

Li, W. 2018. 'Translanguaging as a practical theory of language'. *Applied Linguistics* 39: 9–30.

Lin, A. M. Y. and P. He 2017. 'Translanguaging as dynamic activity flows in CLIL classrooms'. *Journal of Language, Identity and Education* 16: 228–244.

Lin, A. M. Y. and Y. Y. Lo. 2017. 'Trans/languaging and the triadic dialogue in content and language integrated learning (CLIL) classrooms'. *Language and Education* 31: 26–45.

Lin, A. M. Y. and Y. Wu. 2015. '"May I speak Cantonese?"—Co-constructing a scientific proof in an EFL junior secondary science classroom'. *International Journal of Bilingual Education and Bilingualism* 18: 289–305.

Markee, N. 2005. 'Conversation analysis for second language acquisition'. In E. Hinkel (ed.), *Handbook of research in second language teaching and learning*. Mahwah, NJ: Lawrence Erlbaum. 355–374.

Markee, N., and G. Kasper. 2004. 'Classroom talks: An introduction'. *The Modern Language Journal* 88: 491–500.

Matsumoto, Y. 2018. 'At challenging but "learning" moments: Roles of non-verbal interactional resources for dealing with conflicts in English as a lingua franca classroom interactions'. *Linguistics and Education* 48: 35–51.

Moerman, M. 1988. *Talking culture: Ethnography and conversation analysis*. Philadelphia: University of Pennsylvania Press.

Mondada, L. 2018. 'Multiple temporalities of language and body in interaction: Challenges for transcribing multimodality'. *Research on Language and Social Interaction* 51 (1): 85–106.

Moore, E. and C. Vallejo. 2018. 'Practices of conformity and transgression in an out-of-school reading programme for 'at risk' children'. *Linguistics and Education* 43: 25–38.

Nikula, T. and P. Moore. 2019. 'Exploring translanguaging in CLIL'. *International Journal of Bilingual Education and Bilingualism* 22 (2): 237–249.

Poza, L. E. 2018. 'The language of ciencia: translanguaging and learning in a bilingual science classroom'. *International Journal of Bilingual Education and Bilingualism* 21 (1): 1–19.

Psathas, G. 1995. *Conversation analysis: The study of talk-in-interaction*. Thousand Oaks, CA: Sage.

Richards, K. 2003. *Qualitative Inquiry in TESOL*. Basingstoke: Palgrave Macmillan.

Richards, K. 2006. 'Being the teacher: Identity and classroom conversation'. *Applied Linguistics* 27 (1): 51–77.

Rock, F. 2017. 'Recruiting frontstage entextualisation: Drafting, artefactuality and writtenness as resources in police-witness interviews'. *Text and Talk* 37 (4): 437–460.

Sacks, H. 1984. 'Notes on methodology'. In J. M. Atkinson and J. Heritage (eds.), *Structures of social action: Studies in conversation analysis*. Cambridge: Cambridge University Press. 2–27.

Sah, P. and G. Li. 2022. 'Translanguaging or unequal languaging? Unfolding the plurilingual discourse of English medium instruction (EMI) in Nepal's public schools'. *International Journal of Bilingual Education and Bilingualism* 25 (6): 2075–2094.

Schegloff, E. 1987. 'Some sources of misunderstanding in talk-in-interaction'. *Linguistics* 25 (1): 201–218.

Schegloff, E. 1988. 'Discourse as an interactional achievement II: An exercise in conversation analysis'. In D. Tannen (ed.), *Linguistics in context: Connecting observation and understanding*. Norwood: Ablex.

Schegloff, E. A. and H. Sacks, 1973. 'Opening up closings'. *Semiotica* 7: 289–327.

Seedhouse, P. 2004. *The interactional architecture of the language classroom: A conversation analysis perspective*. London: Blackwell.

Sert, O. 2017. 'Creating opportunities for L2 learning in a prediction activity.' *System* 70: 14–25.

Sidnell, J. 2010. *Conversation analysis: An introduction*. West Sussex, UK: Wiley Blackwell.

Spolsky, B. 2004. *Language policy*. Cambridge: Cambridge University press.

Spolsky, B. and E. Shohamy. 2000. 'Language practice, language ideology, and language policy'. In R. D. Lambert and E. Shohamy (eds.), *Language policy and pedagogy: Essays in honour of A. Ronald Walton*. Amsterdam: John Benjamins Publishing. 1–41.

Tai, K. W. H. 2022a. 'Translanguaging as inclusive pedagogical practices in English medium instruction science and mathematics classrooms for linguistically and culturally diverse students'. *Research in Science Education* 52: 975–1012.

Tai, K. W. H. 2022b. 'A translanguaging perspective on teacher contingency in Hong Kong English medium instruction history classrooms'. *Applied Linguistics*. Epub ahead of print. https://doi.org/10.1093/applin/amac039

Tai, K. W. H. 2023a. 'Cross-curricular connection in an Hong Kong English medium instruction western history classroom: A translanguaging view'. *Language and Education*. Epub ahead of print.

Tai, K. W. H. 2023b. 'Managing classroom misbehaviours in the Hong Kong English medium instruction secondary classrooms: A translanguaging perspective'. *System* 113–135.

Tai, K. W. H. and W. Li. 2020. 'Bringing the outside in: Connecting students' out-of-school knowledge and experience through translanguaging in Hong Kong English medium instruction mathematics classes'. *System* 95: 1–32.

Tai, K. W. H. and W. Li 2021a. 'Constructing playful talk through translanguaging in the English medium instruction mathematics classrooms' *Applied Linguistics* 42 (4): 607–640.

Tai, K. W. H. and W. Li 2021b. 'Co-learning in Hong Kong English medium instruction mathematics secondary classrooms: A translanguaging perspective'. *Language and Education* 35 (3): 241–267.

Tai, K. W. H. and W. Li 2021c. 'The affordances of iPad for constructing a technology-mediated space in Hong Kong English medium instruction secondary classrooms: A translanguaging view'. *Language Teaching Research*. Epub ahead of print. https://doi.org/10.1177/13621688211027851

Tai, K. W. H. and W. Li. 2023. 'Embodied enactment of a hypothetical scenario in an English medium instruction secondary mathematics classroom: A translanguaging approach'. *Language Teaching Research*. Epub ahead of print. https://doi.org/10.1177/13621688231152858

Tai, K. W. H. and C. Y. Wong. 2022. 'Empowering students through the construction of a translanguaging space in an English as a first language classroom'. *Applied Linguistics*. Epub ahead of print. https://doi.org/10.1093/applin/amac069

ten Have, P. 1990. 'Methodological issues in conversation analysis'. *Bulletin de Méthodologie Sociologique* 27: 23–51.

ten Have, P. 2007. *Doing conversation analysis* (2nd ed.). London: Sage.

van Lier, L. 1988. *The classroom and the language learner: Ethnography and second-language classroom research*. London: Longman

Waring, H. Z. 2008. 'Using explicit positive assessment in the language classroom: IRF, feedback, and learning opportunities'. *Modern Language Journal* 92 (4): 577–594.

Waring, H. Z., S. Creider, T. Tarpey, and R. Black. 2012. 'A search for specificity in understanding CA and context'. *Discourse Studies 14*(4), 477–492.

Waring, H. Z. and B. L. Hruska. 2011. 'Getting and keeping Nora on board: A novice elementary ESOL student teacher's practices for lesson engagement'. *Linguistics and Education* 22: 441–455.

Wu, Y. and A. M. Y. Lin. 2019. 'Translanguaging and trans-semiotising in a CLIL biology class in Hong Kong: Whole-body sense-making in the flow of knowledge co-making'. *Classroom Discourse* 10 (3–4): 252–273.

Zimmerman, D. H. and D. Boden. 1991. 'Structure-in-action'. In D. Boden and D. H. Zimmerman (eds.), *Talk and social structure: Studies in ethnomethodology and conversation analysis*. Cambridge: Polity Press.

4 Interpretative Phenomenological Analysis for Investigating the Causes of Classroom Translanguaging

4.1 Interpretative Phenomenological Analysis

I draw on the theoretical and methodological frameworks of IPA to investigate how the teachers perceive their own translanguaging practices at specific moments in the interaction. This can increase our awareness, knowledge, and understanding of the teachers' unique perspectives. IPA is a qualitative approach developed within the field of psychology for investigating personal lived experience (Smith, 1996). Smith and Osborn (2008) state that IPA focuses on the in-depth exploration of personal experience and how individuals understand and make sense of their experiences. The assumption behind this idea is that individuals are actively engaged in the world and are constantly reflecting on their experiences in order to perceive them (Smith et al., 2013). IPA has three key theoretical underpinnings: phenomenology, hermeneutics, and idiography. IPA aims to study participants' experience in its own terms rather than overly influenced by external psychological theories or personal proclivities of the researcher. In addition, IPA acknowledges the investigation of the meanings of the participants' experiences as an interpretative enterprise on the part of both researcher and participants. Thus, in order for researchers to understand how participants make sense of their world, a dual interpretation process called 'double hermeneutic' is involved. This requires researchers to try to make sense of the participants trying to make sense of their world (Smith et al., 2013). Due to its nature of in-depth examination of the participants' experiences, IPA is idiographic in the sense that it conducts an in-depth analysis of a small number of participants' experiences. By doing so, it allows researchers to take an 'insider's perspective' (Conrad, 1987) or the emic approach in order to understand the participants' personal experience case by case. This also allows researchers to identify the convergence and divergence,

DOI: 10.4324/9781003351047-4

commonality and individuality within the study sample. Smith et al. (2013) also suggest researchers play an active role in the interpretation process. The active role of the researchers means that various interpretations of the participants' experiences are possible. Given its inductive approach and capacity to explore the participants' complex lived experience, IPA is chosen as the analytical method for investigating why translanguaging practices are constructed in particular moments of the classroom interaction. In the following subsections, the three key theoretical foundations of IPA (i.e., phenomenology, hermeneutics, and idiography) will be explained.

4.1.1 Phenomenology

Phenomenology, developed by Husserl, is a philosophical approach to examine the human experience and 'the way in which things are perceived as they appear to consciousness' (Langdridge, 2007: 10). Husserl argues that a key feature of consciousness is 'intentionality'. In other words, all human experience originates from intentionality, and hence all human actions, thoughts, and feelings have an intended object. This argument challenges the previously accepted understanding that individuals and objects can exist independently (Langdridge, 2007). By exploring these intended objects, one is able to demonstrate how consciousness makes sense of the world as it occurs and in its own terms (Langdridge, 2007). For Husserl, phenomenology entails the careful investigation of human experience. He is specifically interested in searching for a way by which someone might come to accurately understand their own experience of a given phenomenon. This may allow them to distinguish the essential qualities of that personal experience which make it distinguishable from others.

In order for meaning to be explored through experience, Husserl argues that it is necessary to 'go back to the "things themselves"' (Husserl, 1970: 252). The 'thing' refers to the experiential content of consciousness. This is a significant statement since Husserl suggests that individuals often experience the world through using the 'natural attitude'. Put another way, we do not often fully focus on our own experiences and understand them in regard to our pre-existing categorisation system (Smith et al., 2013). Nevertheless, Husserl argues that we should attempt to focus on every specific thing in its own right. Hence, Husserl suggests us to study our experience by adopting a phenomenological attitude rather than a natural attitude. Adopting a phenomenological attitude entails us to 'bracket' our own assumptions and preconceptions. That is, this involves 'bracketing' one's pre-existing expectations and allowing the phenomena to speak for themselves. Husserl refers to this process as 'phenomenological reduction'. The analytical focus is on describing the experience instead of analysing or interpreting the experience according to one's predetermined conceptual criteria. It is, therefore, necessary for a phenomenologist to identify the experience's essential qualities and its underlying meaning. Husserl further argues that through 'bracketing' one's own prejudices and biases, we can investigate the essential meaning of a specific phenomenon (Larkin et al., 2011).

In developing Husserl's work further, Heidegger (1962) introduces a more existential phenomenological approach which moves away from the descriptive commitments of Husserl. Heidegger agrees with Husserl's perspective that an individual's engagement with the world is intentional. Nevertheless, Heidegger argues that individuals cannot be meaningfully separated from their context (i.e., the world of people, objects, language, and culture) (Smith et al., 2013). He argues that the worlds that individuals inhabit are contextually bound and historically situated in a specific life frame, and it is through this perspective that individuals engage with life. Due to these reasons, it is suggested that individuals are not able to fully detach their prior assumptions in order to make sense of their experiences.

Smith et al. (2013) suggest that using phenomenology allows us to understand how we can investigate and perceive human experience in its own right. Husserl has emphasised the significance of engaging in reflective and reflexive thinking when investigating human experience. Nevertheless, I second Heidegger's perspective that we cannot fully 'bracket' our prior experience, knowledge, and preconceptions when studying experience. Hence, the goal of using IPA in this study is to understand EMI teachers' perceptions and their individual experiences rather than identifying the universal 'essence' of the teachers' lived experiences.

4.1.2 Hermeneutics

Hermeneutics is described as the theory of interpretation (Langdridge, 2007). It was originally developed for interpreting biblical texts, but it subsequently developed as a theoretical framework for interpreting various texts, including historical documents and literary texts. In particular, Heidegger (1962) suggests that an individual's engagement with the world and his or her perception of the meaning of his or her experience is accessed through interpretation. Hence, individuals will inevitably draw on their prior assumptions and preconceptions to interpret their lived experiences. Heidegger (1962: 191–192) argues

IPA for Investigating the Causes of Classroom Translanguaging

that 'an interpretation is never a pre-suppositionless apprehending of something presented to us'. Thus, even though our preconceptions will facilitate our understanding of our experience, our preconceptions can also act as a blockade to the process of interpreting our lived experiences where our analytical focus should allow the phenomena to speak for themselves (Smith et al., 2013). This relates to the role of 'bracketing' in the process of interpreting qualitative data (see Section 4.2.1).

IPA operates a double hermeneutic, which means that 'the researcher is trying to make sense of the participant trying to make sense of what is happening to them' (Smith et al., 2013: 36). This requires a high level of interpretation of the part of the researcher (Smith, 2011). Gadamer (1975: 238) argues that 'the important thing is to be aware of one's own bias, so that the text may present itself in all its newness and thus be able to assert its own truth against one's fore-meanings'. In other words, when researchers are interpreting one's experience, it is important for them to be aware of their own preconceptions while analysing the qualitative data. Ricoeur (1970) proposes two approaches for doing interpretation: a hermeneutic of empathy and a hermeneutic of suspicion. A hermeneutic of empathy aims to reconstruct the meaning of the experience from a participant's perspective (Smith et al., 2013). This entails engaging with the data in order to understand what is presented. On the other hand, a hermeneutic of suspicion attempts to search for the hidden meaning in the participant's account of his or her experience. This requires the researchers to employ theoretical concepts from outside the data to explain the psychological phenomena. However, such a deductive approach is not compatible with the approach of this study since this study aims to adopt the emic perspective to reconstruct the phenomena (i.e., teachers' experience in their teaching) in its own terms. Rather, links to theoretical concepts will be considered when the analysis is completed.

Smith (2004) proposes that IPA can integrate a hermeneutic of empathy with a hermeneutic of 'questioning'. This approach allows the researchers to understand a specific phenomenon from the participant's perspective and 'stand in their shoes' (Smith et al., 2013: 36). Alternatively, the IPA researcher should also 'stand alongside the participants' (Smith et al., 2013: 36) in order to ask questions over things that they are saying and make sense of their claims. By doing so, the interpretation may move away from illustrating what the participant would say themselves since it heavily relies on the researcher's interpretation of the experience. Nevertheless, Smith et al. (2013: 36) argue that a successful IPA research 'combines both stances—it is empathic and questioning' and combining both perspectives allows researchers to 'understand both in the sense of trying to see what it is like for someone and in the sense of analysing,

Table 4.1 A set of relationships which can be employed to interpret the data

The Part	The Whole
The single word	The sentence in which the word in embedded
The sentence	The complete text
The complete text	The research project

(Adapted from Smith et al., 2013: 28)

illuminating and making sense of something'. Smith et al. (2013) further state that the interpretations of the individual's experience must always be based on the reading of the data instead of importing a reading from outside the text. Hence, the hermeneutics of questioning differs from Ricoeur's hermeneutics of suspicion because the 'questioning' has to be derived from the reading from within the data itself.

The hermeneutics of the circle is considered as an important concept to IPA. It is concerned with the interactive relationship between the part and the whole at a number of levels (Smith et al., 2013). In order to understand the meaning of any given part, the researcher has to look to the whole. Similarly, the meaning of the whole can only be perceived when the researcher looks to the parts (Smith et al., 2013). This relationship operates at several levels, and the following table is an example of the levels:

This table emphasises the different layers of interpretation as the researcher engages with the text of individuals' experiences. It also highlights that the interpretation process in IPA is dynamic and non-linear, and it requires a repeated process of engagement with the data.

4.1.3 Idiography

The third major influence on IPA is idiography. IPA is different from other psychological approaches which are concerned with making arguments at the group or population level. IPA aims to focus on individual's perspectives and the experiences of specific individuals instead of making population-level claims (Smith, 2004). IPA has a commitment in conducting an in-depth analysis, and subsequently, the analysis has to be thorough and systemic. Since IPA aims to understand specific experiential phenomena from the individual's perspectives, it employs small, purposely selected samples. Idiography can also refer to the commitment to single case analyses or a process that focuses on examining each case before identifying the convergence and divergence across participants (Smith, 2011). For this study, the idiographic commitment will be represented in the analysis chapters by discussing the interview data after the analysis of each classroom interaction extract in order to illustrate the teachers' individual experiences.

It is crucial to note that IPA does not aim to produce generalisable results. Rather it emphasises the idea of 'theoretical generalisability', which refers to the possibility of the research findings to be applied to another context (Hefferon and Gil-Rodriguez, 2011). Smith et al. (2013) argue that IPA invites the readers to play an active role by drawing on their prior knowledge and life experience in order to assess the applicability of the findings and the potential implications for their own practice (Smith et al., 2013). Hence, it is acknowledged that although the teachers' perceptions of their translanguaging practices in the classrooms are only applicable to the teachers under study, the findings can enhance understanding and provide additional insights to the current knowledge base.

4.2 Data Collection and Analysis Procedures

Conducting video-stimulated-recall interviews can allow the researcher and the participating teachers to achieve a shared understanding of the functions of the teachers' own translanguaging practices in the multilingual classrooms. The focus is placed on 'reflections upon descriptions, explanations and justifications given in the course of a talk' (Gellert, 2001: 35) and the teacher's own interpretations of what is happening in the classroom interaction. Speer (2005) points out that using video-stimulated-recall interviews allows researchers to focus on particular examples of teachers' practices; as Speer argues (2005: 224), 'coarse-grain-sized characteristics of beliefs and general descriptions of teaching practices appear unlikely to do justice to the complex, contextually dependent acts of teaching'. Using video-stimulated-recall interviews is also an effective strategy for understanding teachers' beliefs in terms of their pedagogical practices (e.g., Morton, 2012).

IPA can be used to analyse the video-stimulated-recall interview data, and it aims to provide evidence of how the participants make sense of phenomena under investigation and simultaneously document the researcher's sense making. Hence, this requires the researcher to move between emic and etic perspectives. Adopting an emic perspective allows the researcher to analyse the participants' account of experience inductively. On the other hand, adopting an etic perspective requires the researcher to study the data through psychological perspectives and interpret it by applying psychological concepts or theories which the researcher finds useful in demonstrating the understanding of research problems. However, the researcher needs to be careful when applying external theories in interpreting participants' experiences. It is important to remember that all the interpretations must be grounded in the interview data, and this requires a close attention to the interview data itself. As Smith et al. (2013: 37) argue, a successful interpretation is one which is 'based on a reading from within the terms of text which the participant has produced'.

Smith et al. (2013) suggest a number of stages that are involved in data analysis. The analysis entails moving from focusing on the individual to a more shared understanding as well as moving from a descriptive level to a more interpretative level. The following table illustrates the stages which are involved in the analysis (adapted from Smith et al., 2013). It is crucial to note that the analysis is an iterative process rather than linear. This is because the analysis requires the researcher to draw on one's interpretative resources to understand what the participant is saying, but concurrently the researcher is constantly checking his or her own sense-making against what the participant has actually said.

The following analytical stages are followed:

Table 4.2 Stages that are involved in the IPA analysis

Stage	Activity
1 Reading and re-reading	The process involves immersion in the data through reading and listening to the interview recordings multiple times.
2 Developing exploratory comments	This stage entails initial noting on the transcripts in increasing depth. The exploratory comments are divided into the three key areas:
	i **Descriptive comments**: Focusing on the content of the interview and describing the issues regarding the participant's experiences
	ii **Linguistic comments**: Focusing on the participant's use of language
	iii **Conceptual comments**: Providing interpretative comments. In order to develop the interpretative comments, two approaches to interpretations (a hermeneutic of empathy and a hermeneutic of questioning) will be adopted.
3 Moving on to the next case	After analysing the data for a participant, the researcher will move on to analyse the remaining transcripts and repeat the process. Each case is analysed in its own right in order to develop new exploratory comments.

4.3 Research Studies on Using IPA to Investigate Multilingual Practices in Classrooms

To date, there is a small body of research studies that employ IPA as a method to explore the role of multilingual practices in classrooms. To my own knowledge, other than Tai and Li's studies (2020, 2021a, 2021b, 2021c, 2023), there are no other studies that use IPA to understand why translanguaging is employed in multilingual classrooms. In this section, I am going to refer to three research studies that utilize IPA to analyse the teacher's or student's interview data which explores the participant's perceptions about multilingualism in school settings.

Finch et al. (2020) explore how the introduction of statutory inclusion of modern foreign languages (MFL) teaching at Key Stage 2 has an effect on teachers implementing the curriculum in multilingual classrooms in the United Kingdom. The authors first make use of questionnaire data to identify suitable teachers to participate in the in-depth semi-structured interviews. The authors have selected six teachers; these teachers have been involved in MFL teaching at Key Stage 2, and they have relevant experience in teaching English-as-additional-language students and monolingual students. The authors identify two superordinary themes, which include 'MFL delivery as an inconsistent feature of school life' and 'multilingual classrooms as a platform for augmented MFL provision' (p. 6). A range of subordinate themes have also been developed, and this includes 'MFL as a levelling dynamic in the multilingual classroom', 'the impact of subject hierarchy on MFL delivery', and 'the effect of a training void on MFL delivery' (p. 6). The authors suggest that the packed curriculum in primary schools has a negative impact on the MFL provision and MFL does not have equal status as other subjects, such as literacy and numeracy. Hence, it is necessary for educators and policymakers to address such an issue at both a national and local level.

Howard's et al. (2019) study is the first of its kind to explore the school experience of bilingual children on the autism spectrum in the UK. The authors conduct interviews with 11 children on the autism spectrum and of ages between 7 to 14 from across England and Wales. The questions focus on five domains of school experience, which includes 'language use', 'socialisation', 'accomplishment', 'motivation', and 'environment'. The study employs computer-assisted interviewing to elicit students' lived experiences. This is done through showing images on a computer screen, which reflects certain aspects of the domains of school experience. The authors have developed two superordinate themes, which are 'identity formation' and 'experiences of the classroom'. The first superordinate theme, 'identity formation', refers to the students' self-reflections on their identity as being bilingual. The second superordinate theme, 'experiences of the classroom', refers to students' perspectives of their learning environment. The authors argue that children who are educated in a school environment with a larger multilingual population tend to hold more positive views about multilingualism than those who are educated in more monolingual educational settings. The authors suggest schools to create opportunities for students to develop their linguistic identities, which may lead to a positive impact on their school experiences.

In another study, Ho and Tai (2020) conduct semi-structured interviews with two online English teachers and make sense of how they 'do expertise' multimodally and multilingually. Such a research context differs from physical face-to-face classroom setting. The focus on online teaching is also most relevant in the current climate of the COVID-19 pandemic which has resulted in a drastic shift towards online learning on an unprecedented scale. Nevertheless, there is a lack of studies that show how language teachers can strategically use multilingual and multimodal resources to demonstrate their expertise in teaching online. We argue that the concept of expertise comprises three interconnected constructs that constitute expertise in online language teaching. This includes the following: multimodal design knowledge, pedagogical knowledge, and linguistic knowledge. This paper adds to our understanding how the multimodal nature of teaching via video lessons is being articulated by online language teachers. We argue that when creating language teaching videos, online teachers as designers of learning environments have to assess the affordances of online videos and to select apt modes for meaning-making, as different modes have different potentials for meaning-making in their specific contexts of use.

As demonstrated, the findings of the studies use IPA as the methodological framework to illuminate the 'insider' accounts of classroom participants' perspectives about multilingualism in classroom settings. There is a need for research studies to employ IPA to elicit classroom participants' lived experiences of translanguaging in the classroom. Using double hermeneutic as the analytical perspective affords the researchers an opportunity to try to make sense of how the classroom participants make sense of their classroom experiences. Such a methodology can be used to understanding the intricacies of the classroom participants' communicative practices in different contexts.

4.4 Limitations of Interpretative Phenomenological Analysis

IPA aims to collect participants' insights on experience, and this requires researchers to repeatedly listen and analyse the language that the participants employ to make sense of their experiences. Hence, this relies on the ability of the participants to articulate their thoughts. Nonetheless, Willig (2013) suggests that some participants may not have the skills to articulate the intricate details of experience, particularly when they are not familiar with talking in such a way. Smith et al. (2013: 194) further argue that 'our interpretations of experience are always shaped, limited and enabled by language' and this presents another limitation since language is limited in itself. Language may construct barriers to be able to fully articulate our thoughts (Jaegar and Rosnow, 1988).

Additionally, several methodological approaches, such as Discursive Psychology, promote analysing language as a way to perceive how participants discursively construct their 'reality'. Willig (2013) further suggests that researchers can only understand how individuals talk about their experiences through language instead of having an understanding of the actual experience. Nevertheless, Smith and Osborn (2008) suggest that there is a direct connection between how individuals talk about their experience and their thoughts and feelings. The researcher analyses the participant's talk in order to understand how participants make sense of their experiences (Smith, 2011). Although this study acknowledges the limitation outlined by Willig (2013), this study will adopt the perspective that the researcher can learn something about the participants' lived experiences through analysing their language and that the participants can in part describe their experiences.

Moreover, IPA does not aim to explain why participants experience particular phenomena in specific ways. Rather, IPA aims to describe, illuminate, and understand individual's views. Willig (2013) suggests that this is a potential limitation since the lack of explanation can prevent us from understanding the phenomena that the participants have experienced. Finally, it is possible that the interpretations are limited by the researcher's ability to interpret the data as the researcher plays a major role in the process of interpretation (Brocki and Wearden, 2006). In order to ensure the validity of my analysis, some security is offered by the detailed guidelines and discussion in relation to the interpretative process (e.g., Smith et al., 2013, see Section 4.3). The developing analysis includes reading and re-reading the interview transcript and developing exploratory comments (descriptive comments, linguistic comments, and conceptual comments).

4.5 Summary

In this chapter, a detailed overview of the theoretical foundations of IPA is explained. I have also explained the data collection and analysis procedures for analysing interview data. Since there is a lack of research studies that utilise IPA to explore the role of translanguaging in multilingual classrooms, I have referenced studies that employ IPA to understand the role of multilingualism in affecting teachers' and students' perceptions of their classroom experience. Moreover, criticism and limitations of IPA for analysing interview data are explained. Although IPA has its own limitations, it is suggested that IPA is a useful methodology for researchers to take an insider's perspective for understanding the participants' lived experience. Studies by Tai and colleagues (Tai and Li, 2020, 2021a, 2021b, 2021c, 2023; Tai 2022a, 2022b, 2023a, 2023b; Tai and Wong, 2022) have shown how IPA can be employed to review the complexities of teachers' translanguaging practices in Hong Kong English Medium Instruction classrooms. These studies will be discussed in the following chapter.

The next chapter explains how MCA and IPA can be combined together in order to illuminate how classroom teachers can bring in various linguistic, multimodal and spatial repertoires and different sociocultural and pedagogical knowledge for constructing different translanguaging spaces in order to achieve their pedagogical goals and promote content learning.

References

Brocki, J. M. and A. J. Wearden. 2006. 'A critical evaluation of the use of interpretative phenomenological analysis (IPA) in health psychology'. *Psychology and Health* 21: 87–108.

Conrad, P. 1987. 'The experience of illness: Recent and new directions'. *Research in the Sociology of Health Care* 6: 1–31.

Finch, K., A. Theakston, and L. Serratrice. 2020. 'Teaching modern foreign languages in multilingual classrooms: An examination of Key Stage 2 teachers' experiences'. *The Language Learning Journal* 48 (5): 628–642.

Gadamer, H. 1975. *Truth and method* (Trans. G. Barden and J. Cumming). London: Sheed & Ward.

Gellert, U. 2001. 'Research on attitudes in mathematics education: A discursive perspective'. In M. van den Heuvel-Panhuizen (ed.), *Proceedings of the 25th Meeting of the International Group for the Psychology of Mathematics Education 3 (PME-XXV)*. Utrecht: Utrecht University. 33–40.

Hefferon, K. and E. Gil-Rodriguez. 2011. 'Interpretative phenomenological analysis'. *The Psychologist* 24: 756–759.

Heidegger, M. 1962. *Being and time* (Trans. J. Macquarrie and E. Robinson). Oxford: Blackwell.
Ho, W. Y. J. and K. W. H. Tai. 2020. 'Doing expertise multilingually and multimodally in online English teaching videos'. *System* 94: 1–12.
Howard, K. B., N. Katsos. and J. L. Gibson. 2019. 'The school experiences of bilingual children on the autism spectrum: An interpretative phenomenological analysis'. *Research in Developmental Disabilities* 87: 9–20.
Husserl, E. 1970. *Logical investigations* (Trans. J. N. Findlay). New York: Humanities Press.
Jaegar, M. E. and R. L. Rosnow. 1988. 'Contextualism and its implications for psychological inquiry'. *British Journal of Psychology* 79: 63–75.
Langdridge, D. 2007. *Phenomenological psychology: Theory, research and method*. Essex: Pearson Education Limited.
Larkin, M., V. Eatough, and M. Osborn. 2011. 'Interpretative phenomenological analysis and embodied, active, situated cognition'. *Theory Psychology* 21: 318–337.
Morton, T. 2012. *Teachers' knowledge about language and classroom interaction in content and language integrated learning*. PhD thesis, Universidad Autonoma de Madrid.
Smith, J. A. 1996. 'Beyond the divide between cognition and discourse: Using interpretative phenomenological analysis in health psychology'. *Psychology and Health* 11: 261–271.
Smith, J. A. 2004. 'Reflecting on the development of interpretative phenomenological analysis and its contribution to qualitative research in psychology'. *Qualitative Research in Psychology* 1: 39–54.
Smith, J. A. 2011. 'Evaluating the contribution of interpretative phenomenological analysis'. *Health Psychology Review* 5: 9–27.
Smith, J. A., P. Flowers, and M. Larkin. 2013. *Interpretative phenomenological analysis: Theory, method, and research*. Los Angeles, CA: Sage.
Smith, J. A. and M. Osborn. 2008. 'Interpretative phenomenological analysis'. In J. A. Smith (ed.), *Qualitative psychology: A practical guide to methods* (2nd ed). London: Sage.
Speer, N. 2005. 'Issues of methods and theory in the study of mathematics teachers' professed and attributed beliefs'. *Educational Studies in Mathematics* 58 (3): 361–391.
Tai, K. W. H. 2022a. 'Translanguaging as inclusive pedagogical practices in English medium instruction science and mathematics classrooms for linguistically and culturally diverse students'. *Research in Science Education* 52: 975–1012.
Tai, K. W. H. 2022b. 'A translanguaging perspective on teacher contingency in Hong Kong English medium instruction history classrooms'. *Applied Linguistics*. Epub ahead of print. https://doi.org/10.1093/applin/amac039
Tai, K. W. H. 2023a. 'Cross-curricular connection in an Hong Kong English medium instruction western history classroom: A translanguaging view'. *Language and Education*. Epub ahead of print. https://doi.org/10.1080/09500782.2023.2174379

Tai, K. W. H. 2023b. 'Managing classroom misbehaviours in the Hong Kong English medium instruction secondary classrooms: A translanguaging perspective'. *System* 113: 1–35.

Tai, K. W. H. and W. Li. 2020. 'Bringing the outside in: Connecting students' out-of-school knowledge and experience through translanguaging in Hong Kong English medium instruction mathematics classes'. *System* 95: 1–32.

Tai, K. W. H. and W. Li 2021a. 'The affordances of iPad for constructing a technology-mediated space in Hong Kong English medium instruction secondary classrooms: A translanguaging view'. *Language Teaching Research*. Epub ahead of Print. https://doi.org/10.1177/13621688211027851

Tai, K. W. H. and W. Li 2021b. 'Co-learning in Hong Kong English medium instruction mathematics secondary classrooms: A translanguaging perspective'. *Language and Education* 35 (3): 241–267.

Tai, K. W. H. and W. Li. 2021c. 'Constructing playful talk through translanguaging in the English medium instruction mathematics classrooms'. *Applied Linguistics* 42 (4): 607–640.

Tai, K. W. H. and W. Li. 2023. 'Embodied enactment of a hypothetical scenario in an English medium instruction secondary mathematics classroom: A translanguaging approach'. *Language Teaching Research*. Epub ahead of print. https://doi.org/10.1177/13621688231152858

Tai, K. W. H. and C. Y. Wong. 2022. 'Empowering students through the construction of a translanguaging space in an English as a first language classroom'. *Applied Linguistics*. Epub ahead of print. https://doi.org/10.1093/applin/amac069

Willig, C. 2013. *Introducing qualitative research in psychology* (3rd ed.). Berkshire: Open University Press.

5 Triangulating Multimodal Conversation Analysis and Interpretative Phenomenological Analysis for Researching Classroom Translanguaging

Examples from Secondary English Medium Instruction Classrooms in Hong Kong

5.1 Translanguaging as an Analytical Perspective and Moment Analysis

Methodologically, adopting translanguaging as an analytical perspective allows researchers to go beyond doing structural analysis to identify the frequent and regular linguistic patterns. That is, researchers need to move beyond looking for patterns with high frequency and regularity, such as the traditional research on language variation and change (e.g., Cheshire and Fox, 2009) and CA research that explores regular sequential patterns in social interactions (e.g., Tai and Brandt, 2018; Tai and Khabbazbashi, 2019a, 2019b). More importantly, the translanguaging perspective redirects the researchers in focusing on how language users break boundaries between named languages and non-linguistic semiotic systems in particular moments of the classroom interaction (Li, 2011, 2018). Hence, this analytical perspective encourages researchers to explore the spontaneity and transient nature of social interaction (Li, 2020). It helps to highlight the multilingual's creative and critical practices in social interactional contexts. In other words, it allows researchers to illuminate how individuals make good use of the affordances of various available social and linguistic resources creatively to transcend the standards of the named languages and the sociocultural norms.

It is important to note that 'translanguaging spaces are interactionally constructed' (Li, 2011: 1225). In order to analyse the

DOI: 10.4324/9781003351047-5

construction of translanguaging spaces and study the creativity and criticality of multilingual practices, this requires researchers to focus on the spontaneous and momentary performances of the speakers. Moment analysis is a methodology which is proposed by Li (2011) for investigating the spontaneous acts of creativity and criticality in everyday social interactions. As Li (2011) argues, a moment can refer to a turning point or a period of time which has a significant impact on subsequent events and developments. Moment analysis is inspired by the concept of procedural consequentiality, which is associated with CA (Schegloff, 1992), and also the concept of double hermeneutic, which is associated with IPA (Smith et al., 2013; see Chapter 4). Moment analysis focuses on what prompts a particular social action at a particular moment of the interaction and the consequence of the action. In this sense, the researcher is concerned with how a specific moment of the use of various linguistic, multimodal, and multisemiotic resources is being noticed or remarked upon by the participants and what may have resulted in a particular action at a specific moment of the interaction (Li and Zhu, 2013). Using moment analysis allows researchers to explore how speakers manipulate and orchestrate multiple resources to challenge the structural boundaries of named languages and create translanguaging spaces for the act of translanguaging.

Conducting moment analysis requires researchers to collect different types of data sources (Li, 2011). As Li (2011) suggests, it is particularly important for researchers to collect both the observation and audio/video recordings of naturally occurring interactions and metalanguaging data, which are the speaker's commentaries on their own language practices. It is necessary to collect metalanguaging data since it enables researchers to highlight the process of the speakers trying to make sense of their experience as they reflect on their own linguistic performances by themselves or with other interlocutors. The metalanguaging data can be collected through individual or group interviews, journals, or autobiographies. When analysing the data, the researcher needs to focus on the way that the speakers articulate and position themselves during their metalanguaging process. In doing so, researchers can identify any changes in the course of their reflection and themes that emerge from the metalanguaging.

Recent research studies have adopted translanguaging as an analytical perspective to reconceptualise interactional features in specific moments of classroom interaction. Tai (2022b) explored how an English Medium Instruction (EMI) secondary history teacher mobilized diverse linguistic and semiotic resources to contingently respond to the unscripted events in the classroom, including lack of student responses and uninvited student initiatives. It is argued that the process of how the teacher contingently responds to the unexpected outcomes that arise in real-time classroom interactions is a process of translanguaging. Such a process expands the teacher's choice and agency for utilising diverse linguistic and multimodal resources for constructing his pedagogical actions on the spot, instead of having it planned in advance. On the other hand, Tai and Wong (2022) offer a highly interesting and unique study in terms of contextualising translanguaging space in an English as an L1 classroom in the United States. The study focuses on how a native English-speaking teacher constructs a translanguaging space to develop native English-speaking students' English learning. Although the teacher is expected to use English as the linguistic code and develop students' L1 English literacy skills, the teacher implements translanguaging strategically to achieve specific pedagogical goals to enhance students' learning experience. This included enriching her students' language repertoire, enhancing their horizons with diverse sociocultural knowledge and linguistic and cultural practices, as well as cultivating their willingness to appreciate differences and learn new knowledge from others. We argue that the teacher's construction of a translanguaging space has a transformative effect on students' learning since it transforms the ways in which students view languages as resources for communication and appreciate linguistic and cultural diversity in the community.

Additionally, I have demonstrated that adopting a translanguaging perspective in analysing the classroom data can allow researchers to reveal how a multilingual classroom can be transformed into multiple translanguaging subspaces which afford teachers and students to construct new configurations of pedagogical practices. Research studies by Tai and Li (2020, 2021a, 2021b, 2021c) and Tai (2022a, 2022b, 2023a, 2023b) have demonstrated that adopting a translanguaging perspective in analysing EMI classroom interactions can highlight translanguaging as a critical source for creating multiple translanguaging subspaces for content learning and student participation. Tai and Li (2021a) illuminate the potential of playful talk in transforming the EMI classroom into a translanguaging space, which allows the teacher to bring in various linguistic and multimodal resources and different kinds of knowledge to perform a range of creative acts for facilitating content learning and promoting meaning communication. Alternatively, Tai and Li (2020) illustrate the ways an EMI mathematics teacher constructs an integrated translanguaging space by bringing the students' everyday life space into the EMI institutional learning space in order to turn the classroom into a lived experience. This allows the teacher and students to bring their funds of knowledge to the forefront, which makes the content knowledge more relatable and relevant to the students' everyday life experience. In addition to bringing non-academic 'real-life' experience into the classroom, Tai (2023b) reveals how a translanguaging classroom space can be created in EMI history lessons for activating students' prior learnt academic knowledge from other subject areas for supporting students' learning of new academic knowledge. Tai's (2023b) study offers a more dynamic picture of how translanguaging enables EMI teachers to transcend disciplinary boundaries and make a cross-curricular connection in order to deepen students' content learning. Based on the same data set, Tai and Li (2021b) argue that translanguaging creates a space for co-learning, and co-learning allows the teacher and students to learn from each other, which facilitates equity in knowledge construction and recognises students' various knowledges in the classroom. Moreover, Tai and Li (2021c) reveal that the EMI classroom can be transformed into a technology-mediated space where a technological device can extend the teacher's semiotic and spatial repertoires for accomplishing content teaching and promoting student involvement in the classroom. Another study by Tai (2023a) has investigated how EMI mathematics and history teachers mobilise different resources and sociocultural knowledge to address the moments when students produce socially unacceptable and inappropriate behaviour in regard to the normative expectancies in the EMI classrooms and how teachers interpret their actions in managing students' violation of classroom rules. The study provides examples of EMI teachers adopting translanguaging practices in managing student misbehaviours by (1) engaging in playful talk and (2) relying on multimodal resources to cast a stern look and pause instruction and (3) employing verbal cues to redirect students to the content of the lesson. Tai (2023a) argues that EMI teachers can draw on diverse linguistic, paralinguistic, and multimodal resources to address student behaviours which transgress norms for classroom participation. This facilitates the creation of a safe translanguaging space for classroom participants to resume the forward progression of classroom activity. Such a translanguaging space can also be used to maintain control and ease the tension between the teacher's authority and students' participation in the EMI classrooms.

5.2 Issues with Triangulating MCA Findings with IPA

The combination of MCA with IPA is distinct from a 'pure' CA approach, which aims to 'explicate the endogenous organisation of talk-in-interaction as such' (ten Have, 2001: 3), in that it draws on ethnographic information gathered from classroom observations, formal semi-structured interviews, informal interviews, and video-stimulated interviews from participants to triangulate with the classroom interaction analysis. The main reasons why collecting ethnographic information is necessary are the following. First, the interview data gained from the participants and my own perspective as a participant observer can lead to broader interpretations, which allows for the data to be triangulated and offers multiple interpretations of the roles of translanguaging in the EMI classrooms. Importantly, gaining ethnographic information, such as the participants' language attitudes, background, beliefs in teaching and learning, and their own interpretations of the classroom interactions through interviews, is important in understanding how and why translanguaging is employed in specific moments of the classroom interactions, which is not accessible through a description of interactional sequence alone. Second, since translanguaging practices entail multilinguals who 'bring together different dimensions of their personal history, experience and environment, their attitude, beliefs and ideology, their cognitive and physical capacity' to facilitate their meaning-making processes (Li, 2011), MCA cannot reveal how participants bring various dimensions of personal history, ideologies, beliefs, and so on to create the translanguaging spaces in EMI classrooms (Tai, 2021a; Tai, 2022a). These sociocultural factors may not emerge from the MCA analysis directly, but they can be explored through using interviews and/or an ethnographic approach. In short, ethnographic information gained through interviews and participant observations should be integrated with a detailed description of the moment-by-moment analysis of talk-in-interaction. Figure 5.1 visually summarises the methodological approach of combining MCA and IPA. As shown, MCA enables researchers to explore how translanguaging practices are constructed by speakers through their deployment of diverse multilingual, multimodal, and multisensory resources. On the other hand, IPA allows researchers to understand how speakers make sense of their own translanguaging practices. Both research methods adopt the emic approach, which requires researchers not to bring prior assumptions or theories to interpret the ethnographic data.

70 *Triangulating MCA and IPA for Researching Translanguaging*

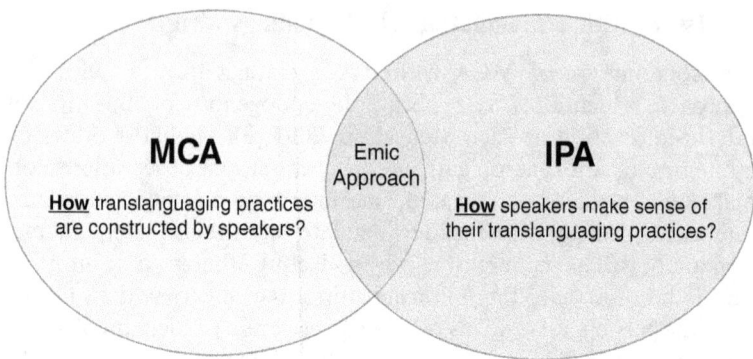

Figure 5.1 Combining multimodal conversation analysis (MCA) with interpretative phenomenological analysis (IPA).

However, the ethnographic information needs to be treated with caution. First, participants may claim that they do not understand something in the conversation although they display their understanding at the time of recording or vice versa. This is possibly because they may forget or reinterpret the interactional moments with the researcher. In addition, contradictory information from the MCA analysis may emerge from the interview data. Several MCA scholars (e.g., Antaki, 2012; Ford, 2012) have offered some arguments for the problems inherent in combining MCA with ethnography. They argue that the goal of MCA is to analyse 'what is publicly transacted, not what is privately thought or felt' (Antaki, 2012: 497). In other words, participants' feelings about the interactions that they participated in have no direct relevance to MCA analysis. This is because MCA analyses do not aim to document the speakers' concerns (e.g., worries, intentions, objectives), which are only knowable to the speakers themselves. The primary aim of MCA is to document the observable resources that speakers employ in constructing their actions in interactions. Second, participants' reinterpretations of their actions are considered as interactional productions which are shaped by the interactional context in which they are produced (i.e., an interview with the researcher) instead of mere representations of the speakers' interests, goals, and so on (Pomerantz, 2012). The participants' reinterpretations of their actions may range from descriptions of the conversations, the speakers' own interpretations of interactional moments, the speakers' own interests, agendas, and concerns, and so on. These various types of reports may or may not be relevant in interpreting what happens in the interaction (Pomerantz, 2012) because they may not be publicly displayed in the social interaction. Third, although Waring et al. (2012: 487) argue that ethnographic information can 'correct an initial MCA analysis with regard to what is being done [...] or what might be inferred', scholars (e.g., Ford, 2012; Pomerantz, 2012) explain that it is not possible to use participants' reports to correct MCA analyses of the talk. This is because MCA aims to capture how participants construct each turn at the moment, and based on the methodological perspective, there are no grounds for correcting MCA analyses of what is publicly displayed through the participants' practices in the talk (Ford, 2012).

Despite the previous arguments regarding the use of ethnographic information to inform MCA analyses, Seedhouse (2004) argues that it is still possible to combine MCA with an ethnographic approach to the study of classroom interaction. Ford (2012: 511) further points out: 'for non-CA research agendas in which CA is used as one method', participants' self-reports are sources for understanding their concerns, ideologies, and the potential links between the retrospective recalls and the real-time interactions. For studying research topics like translanguaging practices, gathering ethnographic information makes absolute sense (Li, 2014) to complement the MCA analysis of the classroom interactions. Seedhouse suggests that an initial MCA analysis of how participants perform an action in interactions can be followed by an ethnographic analysis of why participants perform such an action. However, the methodological imperatives explained by Schegloff (1992) suggest that MCA researchers need to ground the analysis *in the first instance* in the fine-grained details of the discourse, rather than in the external aspects of cultural, social, or personal identity or social context which may or may not potentially be related to that moment of the interaction. Hence, Seedhouse (2004) concludes that although combining MCA and ethnographic information can allow researchers to link the macro-levels of contextual and social structures with the micro-level of linguistic practices, any analytical claim about the interactions needs to be based on the participants' orientations as evidenced in the details of the talk. In other words, the external/contextual factors, such as culture, are relevant to the MCA analysis only if they are demonstrated to inhabit the details of the interaction.

5.3 Data Collection and Analysis Procedures: Combining MCA with IPA

The EMI lessons were video-recorded for analysing classroom interaction data. One video camera was set up in classrooms taught by the teachers in order to capture the teachers' and students' behaviour simultaneously. The camera was located in the back of the classroom, which captured a teacher's view. During classroom observation, detailed field notes were taken. The contents of the fieldnotes entail the following information: the number of students who attended the classes, the students' seating arrangements, the general atmosphere of the classroom, the relationships among students, teachers' and students' unique behaviours and utterances, their attitudes to classroom activities, and most importantly, the specific instances that I identify as translanguaging practices. Such a long-term observation and constant reflections through taking fieldnotes allow me to identify key translanguaging practices in particular EMI classroom moments.

Video-stimulated-recall interviews were conducted with the participating teachers. Before conducting the interviews, video clips which reveal salient features of teachers' translanguaging practices were chosen by me as the stimulus. The teachers were asked to watch the selected video clips and explain why they employed translanguaging practices in those particular EMI classroom moments. This provides the teachers with a chance to reflect on their own pedagogical practices and offer me an opportunity to verify certain things that are not clear from the observation alone. This can illuminate how EMI teachers' translanguaging practices are influenced by various sociocultural dimensions. It also allows me to identify similarities and differences between my own interpretations and their retrospective views regarding the functions of their translanguaging practices and to conduct member-check with them. Each interview took approximately 60 minutes, depending on how many instances were to be discussed during one session. The interviews were conducted in the researcher's and teachers' L1 (Cantonese). However, they were free to use English (L2) to express their thoughts.

Alternatively, in order to ensure the reliability of the data and avoid the teachers forgetting about what was going on at particular interactional moments, I conducted the video-stimulated-recall interviews during the same semester as soon as possible after the translanguaging practices were identified. This is because identifying translanguaging practices normally required a couple of weeks for me to conduct the initial analysis at the latest. It is possible that the teachers might forget why they translanguage in particular moments of the interaction at the time of the interviews. Nevertheless, I still value their own views and their reinterpretations about their purpose for translanguaging, which can potentially open up alternative views or interpretations on the functions of teachers' translanguaging in specific EMI classroom moments in achieving the pedagogical goals of the classroom interactions.

After conducting line-by-line analysis of the classroom interaction data (see Chapter 3 for further details), ethnographic information, such as the information of participants' backgrounds and other wider sociocultural factors, is incorporated with the close descriptions of the translanguaging sequences since the ethnographic information might be inaccessible through the MCA analysis. This allows researchers to understand how and why the teachers' translanguaging practices are influenced by various sociocultural factors, such as personal history, identity, and social contexts. However, the combination of ethnographic information with MCA analysis of translanguaging sequences needs to be treated with caution. In order to ensure that the MCA analyses are not affected by the ethnographic information gained from participants as well as my own perspective as a participant observer, I ground the analysis of the video data in the first instance in the details of the interaction, instead of the external details of the sociocultural factors. The data analysis should be based on the participants' orientations, and any analytical claims should be evidenced in the details of the interaction. However, contextual information can only be analysed in the talk, only when they are 'actually procedurally relevant to the participants at that moment' (Seedhouse, 2004: 91). After completing the MCA analyses, I then analyse the fieldnotes, pre-interviews, and video-stimulated-recall-interview data so that it allows for the data to be triangulated. This can provide different interpretations of the functions of translanguaging practices in particular classroom moments.

After conducting the IPA analysis, I design a table with four columns which assist readers to understand how the analyst makes sense of the teachers trying to make sense of their own teaching. From left to right, the first column presents the classroom interaction transcripts. The second column includes the video-stimulated-recall-interview transcripts. The third column illustrates the teachers' perspectives of their own pedagogical practices. Finally, the fourth column documents the analyst's interpretations of the teachers' perspectives, which aligns with IPA's interpretation process (see Section 5.6 for more information).

5.4 Introduction of the ESRC-Funded Doctoral Project

Adopting English as a second or foreign language other than the learner's first language as the medium of instruction in academic subjects is increasing worldwide. Recently, such a practice is challenged by linguists who argue that the knowledge of other languages that th learners already have plays a crucial role in learning and that translanguaging can facilitate content learning. Translanguaging refers to the exploitation of multiple languages and semiotic resources in the multilinguals' repertoires. Yet there is limited research on translanguaging as a pedagogy in content classrooms, as well as on EMI teachers' reflections on their translanguaging practices. My doctoral research project, funded by the Economic and Social Research Council (ESRC), entails a linguistic ethnographic investigation in Hong Kong (HK) EMI secondary mathematics and history classrooms. HK is a uniquely suitable context for this study because English, being the official language in the colonial era and a current international language, is economically valued in HK's society, and there is a strong preference for EMI among parents and students. Observations with fieldnotes, ethnographic interviews with teachers and other stakeholders, and video recordings were collected in HK. The methodological combination of MCA and IPA involves observing participants' pedagogical practices over time as well as understanding the teachers' reflections on classroom practices. The findings can offer an empirical basis for developing translanguaging as an alternative approach to current EMI policy and practice and discovering the classroom conditions required for the translanguaging practices to succeed. This allows teachers to employ translanguaging to achieve their pedagogical goals, bridge communication gaps, and empower the students.

5.5 Findings from the ESRC-Funded Doctoral Project

In this section, I will present two examples of how EMI teachers in HK utilise translanguaging practices to achieve their pedagogical goals. The first example (Section 5.6.1) reveals how the EMI mathematics teacher creates a translanguaging space through engaging in playful talk in order to engage students in learning mathematics. The second example (Section 5.6.2) illustrates how the EMI history teacher creates a translanguaging space for co-learning. Such a space affords both the teacher and students to learn new knowledge from each other.

5.5.1 Constructing Playful Talk in an EMI Mathematics Classroom

Before presenting the data extract, it is necessary for me to provide some information about the school context and information about the mathematics teacher and students to the readers. The school is a prestigious secondary school in the New Territories, and it is the first EMI school in the local district. The school is a typical local EMI secondary school, which provides education from secondary one to six based on the curriculum guides set by the HK Education Bureau. The school uses English to deliver most of the lessons (except Chinese, Chinese history, liberal studies, and Mandarin classes), and the school examinations are assessed through English. During the fieldwork period, I observed a year 10 class taught by the mathematics teacher over two weeks. The year 10 class was classified as an elite class (based on the school's internal examination results), and all students spoke Cantonese as their L1s. There were 30 students in the year 10 class, and all students passed the internal school English examinations. The teacher has at least eight years' experience in teaching mathematics in English at the school. The teacher is an L1 speaker of Cantonese and previously attended an EMI school for his own secondary education. English is his L2, and he has a limited level of Mandarin proficiency. His bachelor's degree in mathematics and IT education and MSc in Mathematics were obtained from two top-ranked EMI universities in HK.

Extract 1

This extract illustrates how the teacher creatively appropriates student 13's playful comment to draw students' attention to the mathematical terms. It can be seen as playful talk is integrated into the teaching of content-relevant topic (Tai and Li, 2021a). Prior to the extract, the teacher was explaining the mathematical question, which required students to find the number of children using the quadratic equation. While the teacher was explaining, he mistakenly pronounced the word 'children' as /ˈtʃɪl.dən/ (i.e., missing the 'r' sound), and student 13 identified the teacher's mistake by repeatedly initiating the teacher's wrong pronunciation. However, the teacher ignored student 13's uninvited responses, and he continued to carry out his teaching. In this extract, student 13 interrupted the teacher's instruction in order to challenge his English accent.

```
01 S?: minus
02 (0.5)
03 T: +very good minus (0.7) okay?
      +T nods
04 +(1.0)
   +T writes '—' on the BB
05 T: +冇理由加㗎嘛 (.) 減㗎嘛 okay? is okay?
      ((tr. it is not possible to add right?))
      +T directs his gaze to the students
06 (1.4)
07 T: +so do you know how to construct this kind of table?
      +T walks to the LHS of the BB
08 (1.0)
09 T: so first of all +again (0.4) okay (0.5) revise lah+
                     +T rotates his RH continuously--->
                                                      --->+
10 (0.5)
11 T: +find the number of children+ in the original group
                                  (/ˈtʃɪl.dən/)
      +T points at the sentence 'find the number of children' on the screen --->#1
                                                                               --->+
```

Figure #1

```
12 (0.2)
13 S13: 唉↑=
14 T: =will be the unknown that 1 want to find
```

Part 1

Triangulating MCA and IPA for Researching Translanguaging 77

```
15 (0.4)
16 T:  +that's why 1 set x to be +that unknown=
       +T points at the students
                                  +T points at 'children' on BB #2
```

Figure #2

```
17 S13: =chil chil (0.2) 乜嘢
        (/'tʃɪl/) (/'tʃɪl/)
                                 ((tr. what??))
18 (0.5)
19 T: okay?
20 (0.5)
21 S13: [chil chil chil children]
        (/'tʃɪl/) (/'tʃɪl/) (/'tʃɪl/)  (/'tʃɪl.dən/)
22 T:  [and then +try to find (0.5) something new]
                 +T points at the table on BB #3
```

Part 2

Figure #3

```
23  (0.6)
24  T: related to the question
25  (0.9)
26  T: okay↓
27  (0.2)
28  S13: +(NAME-T)=
        +T looks at S13
29  T: =yes?=
30  S13: =你嗰個印度老師仲有有教你啊
        ((tr. is your Indian teacher still teaching you?))
31  +(1.5)
        +T shifts his gaze to window
32  T: +有啦
        ((tr. no))
        +T directs his gaze to S13
33  (.)
34  S13: 你個教授
        ((tr. your professor))
35  (0.9)
```

Part 3

```
36  T: what's wrong with him?
37  (0.2)
38  S13: 你真係獲得佢真傳=
        ((tr. you really have acquired all the skills from him))
39  Ss: ((giggling))
40  +(0.7)
    +T nods
41  T: thank you very much okay? and=
42  (0.6)
43  S13: =pass 完 ah ha↑
        ((tr. finish))
44  (0.7)
45  T: $the↓ the↓ num↓ber↓ of↓ sweet↑ per↓ chil↓dren↑$ (.) okay?
                                                    (/ˈtʃɪl.dən/)
46  (0.2)
47  Ss: hahaha
48  (0.2)
49  T: +something like that okay?
        +T walks to the middle of the BB
50  (0.6)
51  T: then how to solve this +pro↓blem↑?
                              +T writes '=' on BB
52  (0.5)
```

Part 4

```
53 T:   just like the +previous question (0.4) fractional equation
                     +T points at the '=' sign on BB
54      (0.9)
55 T:   fractional equations (.) we can +convert it to become a
                                         +T rotates his RH
56      (0.7)
57 T:   qua↓dra↓tic↓ e↓qua↓tion?=
58 Ss:  =hahahaha
59      (0.3)
60 T:   okay?
61      (1.1)
62 Ss:  hahahaha
63      (0.3)
64 T:   得唔得先
        ((tr. is it okay))
65      (0.2)
66 Ss:  hahaha
67      (0.2)
68 S13: $掉你出去$
        ((tr. throw you out))
69    +(1.5)
      +T smiling
70 T:   okay? (0.5) >+make it to become quadratic equation<
                    +T enacts a throwing motion (T extends his RH index finger and
                     RH started from behind his right shoulder and then goes upward
                     and forward all the way, arm fully stretched, towards the table on
                     BB)
71      (0.2)
```

Part 5

Note that student 13's talk switches the mode from direct instruction to playful talk micro-context by launching a side-sequence (lines 28–69). After the teacher utters 'okay↓' (line 26) which potentially signals his preparation for the next turn, student 13 utters the teacher's name (line 27), which can be seen as an attempt to open another round of talk. The teacher responds to student 13 by uttering 'yes?' in line 29, which invites student 13 to initiate her question. Student 13 immediately initiates a question in Cantonese, '你嗰個印度老師仲有冇教你啊 *(is your Indian teacher still teaching you?)*' (line 30). During the 1.5-second pause, the teacher directs his gaze to the windows on his left-hand side, possibly thinking about student 13's question. The teacher then responds in Cantonese with a negative response, '冇啦 (no)' in line 32. In line 34, student 13 repairs her question in line 30 by saying '你個教授 (your professor)' in order to specify the status of the Indian teacher. The teacher then employs English to initiate a question to student 13, 'what's wrong with him' (line 36). Student 13 responds to the teacher by making a humorous comment, '你真係獲得佢真傳 (you really have acquired all the skills from him)' (line 38), which immediately leads to laughter from the students (line 39). Here, it is evidenced that student 13 is indirectly criticising the teacher's pronunciation through comparing the teacher with his Indian professor. By doing so, the teacher's pronunciation is considered as the equivalent of Indian English pronunciation. At the same time, this also reflects student 13's implied ideology that accents are placed on a hierarchy, and the Indian English accent is perceived by student 13 as inferior and unintelligible. Although student 13's comment in line 38 can potentially be perceived as offensive, the teacher simply nods in line 40 and utters 'thank you very much okay?' in line 41 to acknowledge student 13's comment. In line 43, student 13 takes the opportunity to make an additional comment using both English and Cantonese. Here, the literal meaning of the phrase, 'pass 完', refers to the completed act of passing something. However, it has a figurative meaning behind this message. Similar to line 38, student 13's comment aims to criticise the teacher's pronunciation by justifying that the teacher has acquired the Indian English accent from his Indian professor. Student 13 bursts into laughter, 'ah ha↑' afterwards as she treats her comment as laughable. However, other participants in the class have not treated this moment as laughable as indicated in the 0.7-second pause in line 44.

From lines 45–57, it is noticeable that the teacher is not offended by student 13's sarcastic statements regarding his 'Indian-like' English accent. Rather, the teacher uses this as an opportunity to create a jocular learning environment for students. In line 45, the teacher appropriates an Indian-like English accent to read out part of the mathematical question. As evidenced in line 45, the teacher alters his intonations throughout his utterance: 'the↓ the↓ num↓ber↓ of↓sweet↑per↓ chil↓dren↑'. Such an intonation pattern is audibly different from how the teacher usually pronounces English in class. For instance, the teacher adopts a normal intonation when uttering 'the↑ num↑ber↑ of↓ chil↑dren↓' in line 11. This translanguaging practice allows the teacher to construct a performance of Indian-like English accent in response to student 13's sarcastic comments. The smiley voice in line 45 also shows the teacher's own treatment of his pursuit as somewhat playful. Not surprisingly, the teacher's imitation of an Indian-like English accent is received with laughter from the class (line 47).

After a 0.6-second pause (line 50), the teacher subverts the intonation again when uttering 'pro↓blem↑' (line 51) to elicit responses from students. Normally, the teacher pronounces the word 'pro↑blem↓' with rising intonation in the first syllable and falling intonation in the second syllable. Since no student responds to the teacher's question in line 52, the teacher then provides the explanation to students using his normal tone in lines 53–55. Note that after a micro-pause in line 55, the teacher utters 'we can convert it to become a'. Here, it becomes clear that the teacher's utterance is considered as a designed-incomplete utterance since the teacher invites students to complete the utterance for the teacher. As no one responds in line 56, the teacher provides the answer to students in a playful manner through subverting his intonation, 'qua↓dra↓tic↓ e↓qua↓tion?' (line 57). The teacher's utterance is treated as playful by the students themselves as captured in the laughter in line 58. Although the teacher switches between codes (i.e., English, 'okay?' in line 60, and Cantonese, '得唔得先? (is it okay?)' in line 64) to check students' understanding, students continue to laugh in lines 62 and 66, respectively. It is also noticeable that student 13 utters in Cantonese, with a smiley voice, that she wants to throw the teacher out of the classroom, '$掉你出去$ (throw you out)' (line 68). The teacher is smiling during the 1.5-second pause in line 69 which potentially indicates that the teacher treats student 13's comment as humorous. After initiating a pre-closing 'okay' in line 70, the teacher switches the pace of his talk by speaking quickly, and he asks students to reduce the fractional equation to a quadratic equation. Here, the teacher adopts the 'standard' intonation to pronounce the phrase 'qua↓dra↑tic↑ eq↓ua↑tion↓' which is obviously different from line 57. By doing so, the teacher switches the mode from playful talk back to direct instruction in order to switch the focus on giving mathematical advice to students.

During the video-stimulated-recall interview, the teacher describes his own teaching after watching the video clip. The teacher is invited to reflect on the student's misbehaviour in which a student draws upon a racist stereotype to criticise the teacher's English accent and challenge his face:

Table 5.1 Video-stimulated-recall interview (Extract 1)

Classroom Interaction Transcript	Video Stimulated Recall Interview Excerpt	Teacher's Perspectives	Analyst's Interpretations of the Teacher's Perspectives
36 T: what's wrong with him? 37 (0.2) 38 S13: 你其係攞得我機− 　　　(tr. you really have acquired all the skills from him) 39 Ss: ((giggling)) 40 *T nods 41 T: thank you very much okay? and− 42 (0.6) 43 S13: pass 完 ah ha↑ 　　　(tr. finish) 44 (0.7) 45 T: S the↓ the↓ number↓ of↓ sweet↑ per↓ children↑S (.) okay? 　　　(/ˈtʃɪl.dɹən/) 46 (0.2) 47 Ss: hahaha 48 (0.2) 49 T: *something like that. okay? 　　　*T walks to the middle of the BB 50 (0.6) 51 T: then how to solve this *pro↓blem↑? 　　　　　　　　　　　　　　　*T writes "-" on BB 52 (0.5)	01. T: 哦，教呢啲topics (pause) 我覺得做數嘅時候會有啲悶啊，即係所以咪，加少少有趣嘅嘢成份落去嘛 (tr. Oh. Teaching these topics. (Pause) I felt like it was a bit boring when I was only solving mathematical problems. So that's why I tried to make it more interesting) 02. K: um 03. T: 即係，佢哋，覺得印度，印度式嘅英文有趣嘅喺講下印度式嘅英文，佢哋又聽得明，其實我又唔會影響到佢嘅英文嘅發音，即係我來信唔會影響到佢哋嘅發音，hahaha (tr. That means. They thought that Indian-like English accent was interesting. So, I tried to use Indian-like English accent in my speech. They could understand what I was talking about. And to be honest I won't affect their acquisition of the English pronunciation. That means, I strongly believe that my English accent would not affect their acquisition of English pronunciation. Hahaha) 04. K: hahaha	T's pedagogical goal: encourage students to pay special attention to the mathematical terms.	

53 T: just like the *previous question (0.4) fractional equation
   *T points at the "-" sign on BB
54 (0.9)
55 T: fractional equations (.) we can +convert it to become a
   +T rotates his RH
56 (0.7)
57 T: qua↓dra↑tic↓ e↓qua↓tion?-
58 Ss: -hahahaha
59 (0.3)
60 T: okay?
61 (1.1)
62 Ss: hahahaha
63 (0.3)
64 T: 聽晒將先。
   (Hv is it okay)
65 (0.2)
66 Ss: hahaha
67 (0.2)
68 S13: 9啊你迎岳
   (Hv throw you out)
69 +(1.5)
   +T smiling
70 T: okay? (0.5) >make it to become quadratic equation<
   >T enacts a throwing motion (T extends his RH index finger and RH started from behind his right shoulder and then goes upward and forward all the way, arm fully stretched, towards the table on BB)
71 (0.2)

05. T: 咁所以我就，咪，咪咁樣講囉，好，好願意聽呢個字囉，好似qua↓dra↓tic↓ e↓qua↓tion↑，咪樣嘅呢，即係，但就會，啊，但就會好留心，如果咪平時我就咁樣過就算，但係唔係，哦，但會，但能係，完全係聽過就算，但係唔係，哦，啲pro↓blem↑，咁pro↓blem↓會想聽到pro↓blem↑咁樣，但係嘅係，哦，諗到個兩個字眼但讀咗pro↓blem↑咁樣，即係起碼佢會，唔咪，新嘅佢係可以唔樣做出嚟，唔咪覺原本嘅pro↓blem↓，係啦咁說，嘗試令個堂有咁悶囉佢嘅做得，係得有趣嚟，都係，唔想佢嘅咁悶咁為主，就係咁"
(English translation: So, they would be willing to listen to this word. This means. Like qua↓dra↓tic↓ e↓qua↓tion↑. Something like this. They would be. Oh. They would pay more attention. Otherwise if I simply pronounced it as qua↓dra↑tic↑ e↓qua↑tion↓, they might not pay any attention on it. But no. They. They would. They would want to hear pro↓blem↑ any pro↓blem↑. Oh. Oh. So, the teacher pronounced the word pro↑blem↓ as pro↓blem↑. So at least the students would be able to recognise the 'standard' pronunciation of the two words. So, they would be interested to know how I could do this, and they would also find it more interesting. Yes, that's it. I tried to make the lesson not as boring as possible. Yes, I aimed to prevent boredom. That's it.)

Additionally, he suggested that it could create a jocular classroom atmosphere so that students might not feel bored during the lesson.

Highlighting his deliberate act of imitating a form of pronunciation which was audibly different from the way he usually pronounced English.

T switched the footing by imagining himself as his students and voicing out their reactions

Imitating an Indian-like English accent as a way to draw students' attention and create a humorous classroom atmosphere.

It is noticeable that the teacher switches the footing by imagining himself as his students and voicing out their reactions, '咁pro↑blem↓ 佢讀咗pro↓blem↑咁樣 (Oh. Oh. So, the teacher pronounced the word pro↑blem↓ as pro↓blem↑)' in order to illustrate his belief that the students will notice the teacher's unusual way of pronouncing the English words. Additionally, he suggests that it can create a jocular classroom atmosphere so that students may not feel bored during the lesson. As shown in lines 47 and 58 of the interaction, the teacher's utterances are received with laughter from the students, and they treat these utterances as playful. During the interview, the teacher also compares his normal pronunciations, 'qua↓dra↑tic↑ eq↓ua↑tion↓' and 'pro↑blem↓', with his imitation of Indian-like English pronunciations, 'qua↓dra↓tic↓ eq↓ua↓tion↑' and 'pro↓blem↑'. This highlights his deliberate act of imitating a form of pronunciation that is audibly different from the way he usually pronounces English. As shown, the teacher's pedagogical belief plays a role in shaping his translanguaging practices to construct the sense of playfulness in the classroom in order to achieve his pedagogical goal. By creating a translanguaging space for playful talk, the teacher attempts to disregard the unacceptable behaviour of the student through imitating an Indian English accent.

The researcher is curious whether the teacher has prior exposure to Indian English accent, and the teacher is invited to explain:

01. "K: hahaha 好 (pause) 但係我都覺得好interesting嘅就係，你，你去嘗試去imitate一個accent 出嚟，而嗰個accent 是，你其實識唔識印度口音嗰啲嘢喫，你都係

　　(tr. Hahaha. Right. (pause) But I think the most interesting bit is that you were trying to imitate an accent. And that accent was. To be fair, have you actually learnt Indian-English accent? Or do you simply...)
02. T: 唔識嘅，唔係，但係但係，以前因為，即係大學嘅時候有啲有啲professor印度人嚟㗎嘛

　　(tr. I don't really know Indian English accent. But when I was at university, there were several Indian professors)
03. K: 真㗎？

　　(tr. really?)
04. T: 真㗎

　　(tr. of course)
05. K: hahaha

06. T: 印度Professor，佢哋嗰啲嗰啲terms真係，do↓ you↓ un↓der↓-stand↑ 你係真係完全唔啱音就係印度口音囉，即係，hahaha，佢哋嗰啲
   (tr. Indian professor. Their use of terms is like: do↓ you↓ un↓der↓stand↑. So as long as the intonations are completely wrong then that is considered as Indian accent. Hahaha.)
07. K: hahaha
08. T: 唔同嘅accent你擺唔同嘅位，就會係啱咗囉，係囉就係咁"
   (tr. Arranging different accents into different positions. Then it will be correct. That's it.)

In this interview excerpt, the teacher justifies that he had some exposure to Indian English, and he has identified some features of Indian English when he was a university student listening to an Indian professor's lecturing. It is noticeable that the teacher imitates the way his Indian professor pronounced English words: 'do↓ you↓ un↓der↓stand↑'. His prior exposure to Indian English shapes his belief that as long as the intonations are mixed up in a word or sentences, then it will be considered as Indian English. In this case, the teacher brings in his acquired knowledge of the Indian English accent and appropriates it in the lesson in order to create a humorous effect.

Hence, it is noticeable that the EMI teacher's and students' translanguaging practices adopt specific interactional features, such as appropriating Indian-like English accents, switching between 'standard' and 'non-standard' intonations, and imitating teacher's English pronunciation, which shapes the creation of the playful talk.

5.5.2 Co-Learning in an EMI History Classroom

This extract is extracted from an EMI history lesson which was taught by a teacher at another EMI school. This is classified as a designated school which receives funding from the Education Bureau to deliver a mediated Chinese curriculum for helping South Asian (SA) students in learning Chinese as an L2. The choice of this school as the site of this research is due to the fact that this school has a typical high concentration designated school as 80% of the students are classified as SA students and the school has been educating SA students for an extensive period of time. The majority of the students are from Southeast Asia, and the school has recruited a small group of local and mainland Chinese students. The school provides education from secondary one to six based on the curriculum guides set by the HK Education Bureau.

The school also offers a mixed class in each grade which aims to provide an interactional space where both SA students and Chinese students can learn content subjects together in the same class. This can potentially create a multilingual learning environment for all students where they can engage in intercultural communication.

During the fieldwork period, I observed a year 7 history class, taught by teacher D, which included both Chinese and SA students for over three months. There were 40 students enrolled in the class: 7 of them were Indian, 5 were Nepalese, 3 were Pakistani, 2 were Sri Lankan, 1 was Japanese, 19 were HK Chinese, 2 were Filipino, and 1 was British. All students in this class were 13 years old. The students have received six years of primary education, and they attended primary schools where either English or Cantonese was used as the medium of instruction. The history teacher has taught Chinese language and history for 16 years at School B, and he acts as the head of the history department at the school. The teacher is an L1 speaker of Cantonese, and he is fluent in Mandarin. He recognised that his English proficiency is below average. He previously attended a Chinese-medium-instruction school during his secondary education, and he majored in Chinese language and literature and minored in Chinese history during his undergraduate study in a HK university. He then pursued a postgraduate diploma in education at a prestigious EMI university in HK.

This extract demonstrates more specifically the issue of co-learning of common knowledge that the teacher and student face in classroom interaction. The concept of co-learning emphasizes the process in which teacher and students attempt to adapt to one another's behaviour and learn from each other in order to produce desirable learning outcomes (Brantmeier, 2013; Tai and Li, 2021b).

Extract 2

Prior to the extract, the history teacher was introducing basic information about China, and he drew students' attention to the information on the PowerPoint. At the beginning of the extract, the teacher introduces the fact that China is the third-largest country by reading aloud the text on the screen. The PowerPoint text contains the Chinese translation of the English sentence (i.e., China is the third-largest country in the world).

Extract 2

```
01 T: +okay er china is the: (0.2) third largest country
       +T gazes at the screen #1
```

Figure #1

```
02    (0.5)
03 T: in the world +but who's the first?
                   +T turns his body, facing the students
04    (0.7)
05 T: [and second]
06 SS: [russia]
07    (0.3)
08 T: russia (0.3) second?
09    (1.3)
10 S3: canada
11    (0.4)
12 S4: kind of yeah
13    (0.5)
14 S5: us
16    (0.4)
```

Part 1

```
17 S4: 1 don't know
18    (0.3)
19 S6: canada
20    (0.4)
21 T: +mm: (0.4) yeah (0.2) 1 yeah 1 just search er
      +T places his LH below his chin and he tilts his head #2
```

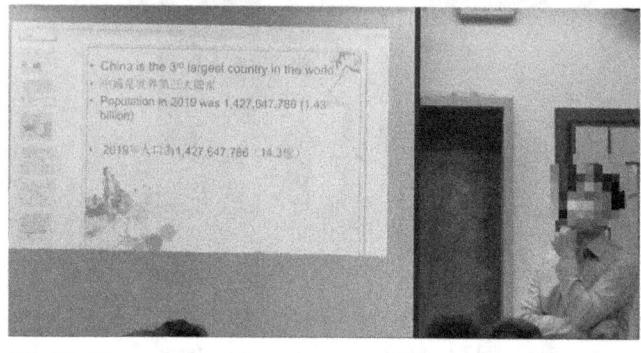

Figure #2

```
22    (0.5)
23 T: er china's the +third
                     +T looks at the screen
24    (0.5)
25 T: +but for the first one and second one mm:
      +T looks at the students
26    (0.2)
27 T: [1'm not sure]
28 S1: [russia is larger]
29    (0.3)
30 S7: russia is the first yeah
```

Part 2

Triangulating MCA and IPA for Researching Translanguaging 89

```
31 (0.2)
32 S8: russia and canada are the=
33 T: =russia shou- russia should be the +top one or top two
                                          +T moves his RH fingers upward
                                             and downward
34 (0.2)
35 T: [+but 1 don't know]
       +T shakes his head
36 S6: [russia is number one ((inaudible))]
37 (0.6)
38 S7: let's search
39 (0.6)
40 T: is um (0.5) india the first?
41 (0.5)
42 S8: what? no: india is just the=
43 T: =+okay +so: +1 just give you a +question
         +T extends his RH and LH arms, palms facing upward #3
           +T closes his hands, fists clenched
             +T opens up his heads again, palms facing upwards
               +T claps his hands
```

Figure #3

Part 3

```
44  (0.3)
45  T: +anyone who can tell me: er the +top one and +top two:
       +T extends his LH, pointing at the students
                                          +T points at the students with his LH
                                           index finger
                                                           +T points at the
                                                            students with his
                                                            LH index finger
46  (0.8)
47  T: +next lesson (0.2) +okay l give you chocolate
       +T turns his head and looks at this RHS
       +T moves his LH to his RHS
                       +T moves his LHS to his RHS, fist clenched as if holding a
                        ball #4
```

Figure #4

```
48  +(0.2)
      +S2 raises up her RH
49  S2: sir l got it
50  (0.3)
```

Part 4

```
51 S7: should be canada
52 (0.3)
53 S2: sir l got it
54 (0.5)
55 T: +yeah you got it?
       +T walks towards S2
56 (0.3)
57 S2: +yeah (.) russia canada and
       +S2 shows her iPad to the teacher
58 +(0.3)
    +T picks up S2's iPad
59 T: oh yeah okay (.) give you chocolate
60 (0.3)
61 T: okay (0.2) l owe you a chocolate okay
62 (1.2)
63 T: what's what's your name?
64 (0.4)
65 S2: (NAME-S2)
66 (0.5)
67 T: +okay um according to (NAME-S2) (0.4) okay
       +T holds up S2's iPad and gazes at it #5
```

Figure #5

Part 5

```
68  (0.9)
69  T: er: (0.8) er: the ((inaudible)) of um
70  (0.4)
71  T: russia canada and china
72  (0.2)
73  T: okay? number one is um russia
74  (0.4)
75  T: number two is um canada
76  (0.5)
77  T: number three is china okay? +1 just er point out china
                                 +T raises up his RH, palm facing students
78  (0.2)
79  T: that's what 1 forgot (.) okay thank you
80  (3.8)
81  T: teacher is +not as clever as er a i
                 +T moves his RH to and fro
82  (1.1)
83  T: okay? maybe ten years later you will have an a i teacher
84  (1.1)
85  T: okay (0.2) +thank you
                  +T returns the iPad back to S2
86  (4.6)
```

Part 6

After introducing the fact that China is the third-largest country (lines 1 and 3), the teacher initiates a question and invites students to think about which countries are the largest and second-largest in the world (lines 3 and 5). This results in several responses from students in line 6, as the students point out that 'Russia' is the largest country. The teacher repeats students' responses by repeating them, and he then utters 'second?' in order to invite students to think about which country is the second-largest in the world (line 8). Several students attempt to offer their answers by saying 'Canada' (lines 10 and 16) and US (line 14). However, the teacher indicates his uncertainty of the students' responses and claims insufficient knowledge (Sert and Walsh, 2013), as indicated in the teacher's truncated response (line 21) and his embodied action of tilting his head and placing his left hand below his chin (Figure #2). Although several students have offered their responses as they say that Russia is the largest (lines 28, 30, 32), the teacher's claims of insufficient knowledge are further exemplified when he utters 'I'm not sure' (line 27) and 'but I don't know' while shaking his head (line 35). In line 40, the teacher initiates a question by asking: 'is um (0.5) India the first?'. The teacher's assumption is challenged by student 8 as he first produces an exclamation "what?" and then offers a negative assessment 'no: India is just the='.

In line 43, the teacher interrupts student 8's speech and attempts to initiate a new sequence. The teacher first extends his right-hand and left-hand arms (Figure #3) and utters 'okay' to draw students' attention. The teacher enacts the same gesture and utters 'I just give you a question'. The teacher then claps his hands as a way to ensure that the students are paying close attention to his forthcoming question. In lines 45 and 47, the teacher specifies the question, which requires students to find out the answer of the first and second-largest countries in the world by the next lesson. The teacher deliberately clenches his fist and moves his left hand to the right-hand-side when he says, "okay I give you chocolate" while figuratively pretending to hold a chocolate in his left hand. By doing so, the teacher potentially aims to motivate students to look for the information after class. In lines 49 and 53, student 2 initiates a claim of understanding as she utters 'sir I got it' twice, which draws the teacher's attention in line 55. Student 2 then shows her iPad to the teacher and confirms her peer's answers: 'russia canada' (line 57). This illustrates that student 2 deploys the iPad as a resource for her to check the accurate answer for the teacher, which in turn, teaches the correct information to the teacher and her classmates. The teacher picks up student 2's iPad (line 58), and he verbally acknowledges student 2's answer by repeating the answers repeatedly in lines 71, 73, 75 and 77. It is noticeable that the teacher verbally acknowledges his knowledge gap by stating "I just er point out china" (line 77) and "that's what I forgot" (line 79). The teacher further makes a comment by comparing himself with artificial intelligence, 'teacher is not as clever as er a i' (line 81), which highlights the limitations of humans' memory capacity.

In this extract, although the whole conversation is carried out in English, the teacher translanguages through his concurrent employment of verbal (use of English) and gestural actions (e.g., extending his arms and tilting his head) in order to claim his insufficient knowledge and invite students in providing the accurate knowledge to him and also to other classmates. It is evidenced that the teacher learns the information about the first and second-largest countries in the world when student 2 looks for the information via her iPad. This demonstrates how student 2 draws on the technological resource that is available to her, and this affords her in informing the correct answer to the teacher. During the video-stimulated-recall interview, the teacher is invited to explain the role of co-learning in shaping the classroom interaction:

In line 2, the teacher first points out the possible solutions for dealing with uninvited student initiatives. One of the ways is to allow students to find out the correct answer and invite them to inform the answer to the teacher and other peers. The researcher then raises another question that prompts the teacher to reflect on the role of co-learning in challenging the teacher's status as a history teacher. The teacher then justifies that it is alright for students to teach him the correct information. It is noticeable that the teacher shifts the footing by imagining himself as his students and voicing out their thoughts: '哦原來你呢個唔知嘅，你呢個係錯嘅 (Oh you don't know that? Oh, you are wrong)'. This shift of footing demonstrates the teacher's own perception of his student's reactions when the teacher indicates a claim of insufficient knowledge. He then metaphorically compares himself with artificial intelligence, and by doing so, the teacher is emphasising the limitations of a human's cognitive system. This is also reflected in the MCA analysis when the teacher explicitly states that 'teacher is not as clever as AI' (line 81). By emphasising the fact that he is a 'human being', the teacher highlights his willingness to co-learn new knowledge with his students.

The teacher further elaborates on his account, and he explains that a classroom is a space for co-learning. The teacher points out that learning is not only one way (i.e., teacher teaching new knowledge to students). Rather, both teacher and students can engage in learning something new from each other. Such a belief is manifested in his account as he says: '咁其實係可以大家一齊學習，咁我又learn一啲野喺佢哋身上，咁佢又learn一啲野喺我身上 (They can learn new knowledge from me, and I can also learn new knowledge from them)'. This belief echoes Brantmeier's (2013) argument that co-learning alters the role sets of teacher and students since the teacher is no longer the only knowledge provider in the classroom. The classroom is then transformed into a space for mutual learning and equal participation for all classroom participants. It can be argued that the teacher's engagement in co-learning is motivated by his pedagogical belief about education and his goal for promoting equal contributions from the students, which result in the creation of a translanguaging space for co-learning in the EMI history classroom.

Table 5.2 Video-stimulated-recall interview (Extract 2)

Classroom Interaction Transcript	Video Stimulated Recall Interview Excerpt	Teacher's Perspectives	Analyst's Interpretations of the Teacher's Perspectives

17 S4: i don't know
18 (0.3)
19 S6: canada
20 (0.4)
21 T: +mm: (0.4) yeah (0.2) i yeah i just search er
+T places his LH below his chin and he tilts his head #2
 	
Figure #2
 	
22 (0.5)
23 T: er china's the +third
                   +T looks at the screen
24 (0.5)
25 T: +but for the first one and second one mm:
    +T looks at the students
26 (0.2)
27 T: [i'm not sure]
28 S1: [russia is larger]
29 (0.3)
30 S7: russia is the first yeah
	01. K: 你覺得你喺學生身上學唔學到嘢啊係呢一個moment? (tr. Do you feel like you have learnt anything from the students at this moment of the interaction?)
	
	02. T: 學到啊，因為無論係History又好或者其他科都好，可能你prepare咁啲嘢，但佢哋知道吖，跟住佢哋提出另外一啲問題，可能你突然之間就比佢哋考起，跟住佢就答唔到，咁你可能其時有時間嘅話可以即刻搵資料啦，諗啦，即刻諗，一諗啦，但係如果當其時有時間嘅話當堂即時嘅話有時間嘅就OK嘅，咁就，即係一係就下一堂同佢講，如果唔係就拋番番個波比佢，即係，即係下一堂嘅話一話畀我聽啊，咁都OK嘅 (tr. Yes, I have. I believe that no matter whether it is History or other academic subjects, you may have to prepare some teaching materials in advance and students may ask you a question that is not covered in the material at all. It is possible that you may not be able to answer that question because you have not encountered that question before. If you have time, you may immediately look for the information and think about it. However, if you do not have time during class, then you may tell the students that we can discuss the question during the next lesson. You can also tell the students to look up the answer by themselves and ask them to tell you the answer in the next lesson. I believe that this approach will work too.)
		T understands that there are times where a teacher may not be able to answer certain questions even though he or she has prepared the teaching material in advance. T proposes two ways for teachers to deal with such situation: 1) use the class time to look for the answer; 2) leave the question to the next lesson.	T believes that it is okay to learn new knowledge from his students

(Continued)

Table 5.2 (Continued)

Classroom Interaction Transcript	Video Stimulated Recall Interview Excerpt	Teacher's Perspectives	Analyst's Interpretations of the Teacher's Perspectives

31 (0.2)
32 S8: russia and canada are the=
33 T: =russia shou- russia should be the =top one or top two
    +T moves his RH fingers upward and downward
34 (0.2)
35 T: (+but i don't know)
    +T shakes his head
36 S6: [russia is number one ((inaudible))]
37 (0.6)
38 S7: let's search
39 (0.6)
40 T: is um (0.5) india the first?
41 (0.5)
42 S8: what? +no: india is just the=
43 T: =+okay +so: +i just give you a +question
    +T extends his RH and LH arms, palms facing upward #3
    +T closes his hands, flats clenched
    +T opens up his hands again, palms facing upwards
    +T claps his hands
 	
Figure #3
	03. K: 你覺得，因為好多時學生會覺得老師係喺個學科人邊嘅expert，但係當一個老師如果唔知道個答案嘅時候呢，但係都嘗試向學生攞資料，係處於一個比較虛心嘅一個嘅態度去向學生學習，你覺得Break through 呢一個social status 對你嚟講有冇影響?
	(tr. Often students may think that teachers are experts. However, when a teacher does not know the answer and attempts to seek for information from students, this requires the teacher to adopt a modest attitude in order to learn from the students. Do you think that by doing so, it challenges your status as a teacher?)
			The researcher is trying to understand why T is willing to learn from his students.

44 (0.3)		
45 T: +anyone who can tell me: or the +top one and +top two: +T extends his LH, pointing at the students +T points at the students with his LH index finger		
46 (0.8)		
47 T: +next lesson (0.2) +okay I give you chocolate +T turns his head and looks at this RHS +T moves his LH to his RHS		
		+T moves his LHS to his RHS, fist clenched as if holding a ball #4
		Figure #4
48 +(0.2) +S2 raises up her RH		
49 S2: sir I got it		
50 (0.3)		
04. T: 有呀，雖然話我識嘅嘢梗係比學生多啦，咁係因為你學嘅時間啦，你嘅年資啦，你年長好多啦，但係我又會覺得學生話比老師聽，哦原來你呢個唔知喎，或者面子個係錯嘅，又唔覺得呀，我自己就覺得你就算係expert都好啦，嘅問題，因為，我自己就覺得你就算係expert都好啦，你都唔係知晒所有嘢喫嘛，咁你知道晒所有嘢咁你就係AI啦，咁就唔需要我吖，我係一個human being，咁可能有時我自己記唔嘢都可能記錯嘅 (tr. Not really. Although I know more than my students due to the amount of exposure that I have received and also my life experience, I don't think that it's a problem for my students to share new information with me. A student may say: "oh you don't know that?" "Oh you are wrong". I will not feel embarrassed or disappointed or feel ashamed. This is because I think that although you are an expert, you will not know everything. If you know everything, you will become an artificial intelligence. In that case, you don't need me at all because I am just a human being and I sometimes will make mistakes or forget certain information.)	T believes that it is alright for students to teach him the correct information. T metaphorically compares himself with artificial intelligence which highlights the limitations of human's cognitive system.	T imitates a student's voice and imagines that the student is criticizing the teacher's incapability in teaching the subject. T's use of metaphor of comparing himself with artificial intelligence is also reflected in the classroom interaction.

(Continued)

Table 5.2 (Continued)

Classroom Interaction Transcript	Video Stimulated Recall Interview Excerpt	Teacher's Perspectives	Analyst's Interpretations of the Teacher's Perspectives

51 S7: should be canada
52 (0.3)
53 S2: sir 1 got it
54 (0.5)
55 T: +yeah you got it?
  +T walks towards S2
56 (0.3)
57 S2: +yeah (.) russia canada and
  +S2 shows her iPad to the teacher
58 +(0.3)
  +T picks up S2's iPad
59 T: oh yeah okay (.) give you chocolate
60 (0.3)
61 T: okay (0.2) I owe you a chocolate okay
62 (1.2)
63 T: what's your name?
64 (0.4)
65 S2: (NAME-S2)
66 (0.5)
67 T: +okay um according to (NAME-S2) (0.4) okay
  +T holds up S2's iPad and gazes at it #5
 	
Figure #5
	05. T: 即係可能，一件歷史事件可能係明太祖嘅，咁可能我就記咗做明成祖，咁如果嗰學生知道嘅，哦唔係呀係明成祖呀，哦sorry呀咁樣，咁所以，你備課嘅時候都要做足功課啦，即係唔係就咁人去就亂吹啦，但係你都要承認嘅就係，即係自己始終都係一個human being呀，咁你係會有啲嘢唔記得嘅，或者你係有一啲嘢你係行學到嘅，咁如果有學生可以回你分享嘅，咁咪一齊learn囉
	(tr. So perhaps when I am teaching a historical event, that event was associated with Ming Emperor Taizu. However, I may mix it up with Ming Emperor Chengzu. If students realise the mistake, they may say "Oh no it's Ming Emperor Taizu". I will then say: "oh sorry!" Of course, it is important for teachers to do preparation work in advance. You cannot just walk into the classroom and say random things. However, you have to admit the fact that you are just a human being, and you may forget certain information. Or there may be something that you have not learnt before. So, when students are able to tell you the answer, then you should learn from them.)
		T gives an example of a scenario when he mixes up the historical facts and how students can correct him.
		
		T admits that he is a human being and he is willing to learn from his students.
			T switches between the student's and teacher's voices in order to showcase how he will deal with such situation.

Transcript	Translation	Comment

68 (0.9)
69 T: er: (0.8) er: the ((inaudible)) of um
70 (0.4)
71 T: russia canada and china
72 (0.2)
73 T: okay? number one is um russia
74 (0.4)
75 T: number two is um canada
76 (0.5)
77 T: number three is china okay? +I just er point out china
   +T mims up his RH, palm facing students
78 (0.2)
79 T: that's what I forgot (.) okay thank you
80 (3.8)
81 T: teacher is +not as clever as er a i
   +T moves his RH to and fro
82 (1.1)
83 T: okay? maybe ten years later you will have an a i teacher
84 (1.1)
85 T: okay (0.2) +thank you
   +T returns the iPad back to S2
86 (4.6)
06. T: 因為其實始終嘅個課堂就係一齊learn囉，咁又行話一定係我單向傳嘅比佢，咁其實係可以大家一齊學習，咁我又learn一啲嘢嚟佢學習，咁佢又learn一啲嘢嚟我身上，呢個就係學習同埋教育呀嘛，咁所以我唔會覺得自己係冇嘢可以學習囉，其實自己都要學
(tr. This is because it is a lesson, and it is a place for teachers and students to learn together. It is not only restricted to the teacher teaching knowledge to students. Both teacher and students can learn something new. They can learn new knowledge from me, and I can also learn new knowledge from them. That's what education and learning are all about. Therefore, I will not think that I have nothing to learn from my students and I understand that I have to learn as well.)
		T's open-minded attitude is the factor that motivates him to co-learn with the students.
		
		T believes that a classroom is a space for teachers and students to engage in co-learning.

5.6 Concluding Remarks

5.6.1 Summary of the Main Themes

In this chapter, I present how the EMI mathematics and history teachers employ various linguistic and multimodal resources not simply to teach content knowledge to the class but also to learn from their students to create a translanguaging space for playful talk (Section 5.6.1) and a translanguaging space for co-learning (Section 5.6.2). The findings have illustrated that translanguaging allows the EMI teachers to employ different linguistic and multimodal resources, and their sociocultural and pedagogical knowledge to accomplish their pedagogical goals at specific moments in the interaction. The study demonstrates that combining MCA with IPA to analyse the classroom interaction is appropriate since MCA allows me to identify examples of the teacher's translanguaging practices. I am able to triangulate my MCA analysis with the IPA analysis of the video-stimulated-recall-interview data in order to understand how and why translanguaging is constructed at that moment of the interaction. By doing so, this enables researchers to expand the linguistic analysis of the classroom talk and capture how participants bring in their funds of knowledge to construct their translanguaging practices in the classroom. The study also highlights the importance of the video-stimulated-recall interviews in order to allow the teacher to reflect upon his own translanguaging practices. The teachers also comment that the interview is a reflective process for them to make sense of their own pedagogical practices.

A key theoretical contribution of the study is that it advances our understanding of the EMI classroom as an integrated translanguaging space, and it entails multiple translanguaging subspaces which afford EMI teachers and students to bring the relevant multilingual and multimodal resources and sociocultural knowledge in achieving a range of pedagogical goals. I have demonstrated the creation of different translanguaging subspaces in EMI classrooms which are created by and created for translanguaging. These include a translanguaging space for playful talk (Section 5.6.1) and a translanguaging space for co-learning (Section 5.6.2). In my doctoral research, I have also demonstrated the creation of a translanguaging space for bringing outside knowledge into the classroom (Tai and Li, 2020; Tai, 2023b), a space for managing student misbehaviours (Tai, 2023a), and a technology-mediated translanguaging space (Tai and Li, 2021c). These translanguaging subspaces allow classroom participants to bring in a range of linguistic and multimodal resources and different kinds of knowledge into the lessons, which can create new configurations of language and pedagogical practices. Creating different translanguaging subspaces within an EMI classroom can also transform the traditionally teacher-fronted interaction to negotiate a space for voicing their thoughts and create a more dynamic and contingent environment to facilitate students' participation (Tai and Li, 2021a; Tai, 2022b).

In the doctoral study, I have demonstrated that the teachers' translanguaging practices are shaped by the teachers' prior life experience, personal interest in adopting particular linguistic features (e.g., Section 5.6.2), various pedagogical knowledge, and beliefs into the classroom interaction, which contributes to the creation of translanguaging subspaces in the classrooms. The project has led to the development of a pedagogical model which allows EMI or CLIL or L2 teachers to identify the social and contextual factors that contribute to the creation of different translanguaging subspaces for achieving specific pedagogical goals in the classrooms. Figure 5.2 illustrates a pedagogical model for creating different translanguaging subspaces in multilingual classrooms.

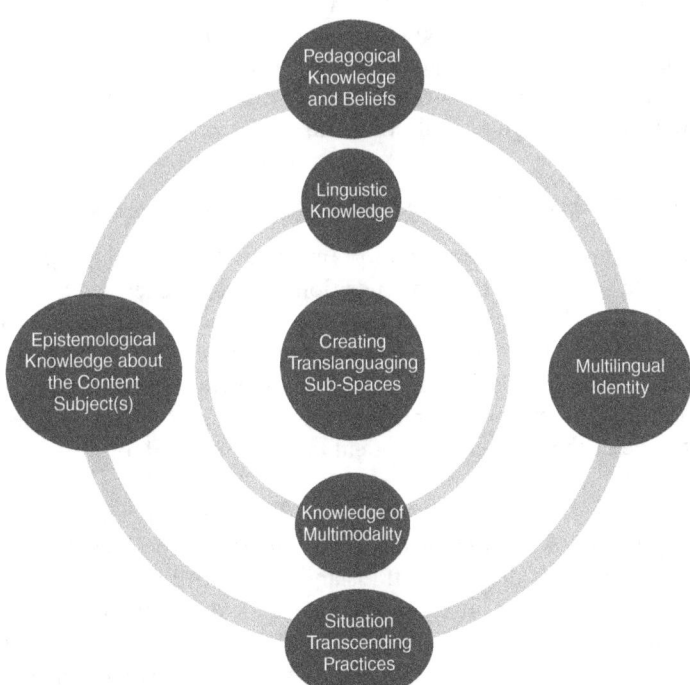

Figure 5.2 Pedagogical Model for Creating Translanguaging Sub-Spaces.

In order for teachers to create a translanguaging subspace, teachers will need to draw on their linguistic knowledge, which includes their awareness of linguistic theories and ideologies. As argued, using the knowledge already acquired through the teachers' first and/or prior learned languages can play an important role in L2 and content learning (Tai and Li, 2021a). Teachers also need to draw on their knowledge of multimodality, which refers to the knowledge of using diverse semiotic resources strategically, such as visuals, gestures, body movements, and online resources. I also argue that in addition to the deployment of multilingual and multimodal knowledge, there are other meaning-making resources for shaping the teacher's deployment of multilingual and multimodal resources in the classroom interactions. This includes (1) situation-transcending practices (i.e., the teacher connects the present teaching or learning situation with past knowledge and experiences), (2) pedagogical knowledge and beliefs (i.e., knowledge and beliefs about teaching approaches, teaching resources, learners' expectations, learning processes, and assessment), (3) epistemological knowledge about the content subjects (i.e., subject knowledge), (4) multilingual identity (i.e., how teachers see themselves as multilinguals and their beliefs about multilingualism). Such a model can enable EMI or CLIL or L2 teachers to plan their translanguaging practices or adapt them flexibly to suit their own teaching contexts. This pedagogical model can be further refined through constant interplay between additional data collection and analysis.

5.6.2 Reflexivity and Positionality of Myself as a Researcher

To conclude this chapter, an important issue related to my subjectivity has to be addressed. First, my position as a researcher and my presence in the EMI classrooms could potentially influence how the teacher and students engage in classroom interactions. It is noticeable that the classroom participants are less attentive to me and the video camera as the semester progressed. However, it is vital to acknowledge that none of the teacher and student talk were elicited for my research purposes.

Moreover, I also recognise that my role as a researcher shaped the research process in different ways, particularly when I was interviewing the teachers, identifying translanguaging instances for analysis, and interpreting the interactional data and video-stimulated-recall-interview data. My positionality as a researcher could have affected how I talked to them, what they shared with me, and what I analyse as relevant data.

These issues are not only restricted to this study since subjectivity is an inherent limitation in qualitative studies. Nevertheless, this study offers in-depth and complex interpretations of different translanguaging practices through MCA analysis and member check by video-stimulated-recall interviews. Additionally, as Stake (1995) argues, subjectivity can be a strength when researchers acknowledge their own bias. Researchers can employ subjectivity as the starting point for understanding a specific phenomenon. Notably, I would like to draw on my subject position as a qualified English-as-a-second-language teacher so that this study can reveal the phenomenon of translanguaging in EMI classrooms from an insider view. In summary, while I understand my subjective position as possible bias, I aim to employ my subjectivity to understand the insider knowledge among the participating EMI teachers and find out multiple realities regarding the teachers' translanguaging practices in the EMI classrooms for achieving their pedagogical goals.

References

Antaki, C. 2012. 'What actions mean, to whom, and when'. *Discourse Studies* 14: 493–498.
Brantmeier, E. J. 2013. 'Pedagogy of vulnerability: Definitions, assumptions, and applications'. In J. Lin, R. Oxford, E. J. Brantmeier (eds.), *Re-envisioning higher education: Embodied pathways to wisdom and transformation* (pp. 95–106). Charlotte, NC: Information Age.
Cheshire, J. and S. Fox. 2009. 'Was/were variation: A perspective from London'. *Language Variation and Change* 21: 1–38.
Ford, C. 2012. 'Clarity in applied and interdisciplinary conversation analysis'. *Discourse Studies* 14: 507–513.
Li, W. 2011. 'Moment analysis and translanguaging space: Discursive construction of identities by multilingual Chinese youth in Britain'. *Journal of Pragmatics* 43: 1222–1235.
Li, W. 2014. 'Translanguaging knowledge and identity in complementary classrooms for multilingual minority ethnic children'. *Classroom Discourse* 5: 158–175.
Li, W. 2018. 'Translanguaging as a practical theory of language'. *Applied Linguistics* 39: 9–30.
Li, W. 2020. 'Multilingual English users' linguistic innovation'. *World Englishes* 39: 236–248.
Li, W. and H. Zhu. 2013. 'Translanguaging identities: Creating transnational space through flexible multilingual practices amongst Chinese university students in the UK'. *Applied Linguistics* 34 (5): 516–535.
Pomerantz, A. 2012. 'Do participants' reports enhance conversation analytic claims? Explanation of one sort or another'. *Discourse Studies* 14 (4): 499–505.

Schegloff, E. A. 1992. 'To Searle on conversation'. In J. R. Searle, H. Parret, and J. Verschueren (eds.), *(On) Searle on conversation*. Amsterdam & Philadelphia: John Benjamins. 113–128.

Seedhouse, P. 2004. *The interactional architecture of the language classroom: A conversation analysis perspective*. London: Blackwell.

Sert, O. and S. Walsh. 2013. 'The interactional management of claims of insufficient knowledge in English language classrooms'. *Language and Education*, 27 (6): 542–565.

Smith, J. A., P. Flowers, and M. Larkin. 2013. *Interpretative phenomenological analysis: Theory, method, and research*. Los Angeles, CA: Sage.

Stake, E. R. 1995. *The art of case study research*. Thousand Oaks, CA: Sage.

Tai, K. W. H. and A. Brandt. 2018. 'Creating an imaginary context: Teacher's use of embodied enactments in addressing learner's initiatives in a beginner-level adult ESOL classroom'. *Classroom Discourse* 9 (3): 244–266.

Tai, K. W. H. and N. Khabbazbashi. 2019a. 'The mediation and organisation of gestures in vocabulary instructions: A microgenetic analysis of interactions in a beginning-level adult ESOL classroom'. *Language and Education* 33 (5): 445–468.

Tai, K. W. H. and N. Khabbazbashi. 2019b. 'Vocabulary explanations in beginning-level adult ESOL classroom interactions: A conversation analysis perspective'. *Linguistics and Education* 52: 61–77.

Tai, K. W. H. and W. Li. 2020. 'Bringing the outside in: Connecting students' out-of-school knowledge and experience through translanguaging in Hong Kong English medium instruction mathematics classes'. *System* 95: 1–32.

Tai, K. W. H. and W. Li. 2021a. 'Constructing playful talk through translanguaging in the English medium instruction mathematics classrooms'. *Applied Linguistics* 42 (4): 607–640.

Tai, K. W. H. and W. Li 2021b. 'Co-learning in Hong Kong English medium instruction mathematics secondary classrooms: A translanguaging perspective'. *Language and Education* 35 (3): 241–267.

Tai, K. W. H. and W. Li 2021c. 'The affordances of iPad for constructing a technology-mediated space in Hong Kong English medium instruction secondary classrooms: A translanguaging view'. *Language Teaching Research*. Epub ahead of print. https://doi.org/10.1177/13621688211 0278

Tai, K. W. H. and W. Li. 2023. 'Embodied enactment of a hypothetical scenario in an English medium instruction secondary mathematics classroom: A translanguaging approach'. *Language Teaching Research*. Epub ahead of print. https://doi.org/10.1177/13621688231152858

Tai, K. W. H. 2021a. 'Researching translanguaging in EMI classrooms'. In J. Pun and S. Curle (eds.), *Research methods for English medium instruction in action*. London: Routledge. 119–132.

Tai, K. W. H. 2021b. *Translanguaging in Hong Kong English medium instruction classrooms: An ethnomethodologically informed study of classroom interaction and teachers' reflection*. PhD Thesis, University College London, U.K.

Tai, K. W. H. 2022a. 'Translanguaging as inclusive pedagogical practices in English medium instruction science and mathematics classrooms for linguistically and culturally diverse students'. *Research in Science Education* 52: 975–1012.

Tai, K. W. H. 2022b. 'A translanguaging perspective on teacher contingency in Hong Kong English medium instruction history classrooms'. *Applied Linguistics*. Epub ahead of print. https://doi.org/10.1093/applin/amac081

Tai, K. W. H. 2023a. 'Managing classroom misbehaviours in the Hong Kong English medium instruction secondary classrooms: A translanguaging perspective'. *System* 113: 1–35.

Tai, K. W. H. 2023b. 'Cross-curricular connection in an Hong Kong English medium instruction western history classroom: A translanguaging view'. *Language and Education*. Epub ahead of print. https://doi.org/10.1080/09500782.2023.2174379

Tai, K. W. H. and C. Y. Wong. 2022. 'Empowering students through the construction of a translanguaging space in an English as a first language classroom'. *Applied Linguistics*. Epub ahead of print. https://doi.org/10.1093/applin/amac069

ten Have, P. 2001. 'Applied conversation analysis'. In A. McHoul and M. Rapley (eds.), *How to analyse talk in institutional settings: A casebook of methods*. London: Continuum. 3–11.

Waring, H. Z., S. Creider, T. Tarpey, and R. Black. 2012. 'A search for specificity in understanding CA and context'. *Discourse Studies*, 14 (4), 477–492.

6 Conclusion

6.1 Methodological Implications

In Chapters 3 and 5, I have demonstrated that MCA offers a detailed analysis of classroom interaction which allows researchers to observe not only the use of different named languages, but also the role of space, objects, and other semiotic features in the interaction. MCA requires researchers to adopt Jefferson's (2004) and Mondada's (2018) transcription systems to include the sequential and paralinguistic elements of the interaction and also descriptions of embodied conduct. Minute detailed transcription is important for us to understand how teachers' translanguaging practices draw not only on linguistic but on spatial and other semiotic resources that make learning accessible for all in multilingual classrooms. This addresses Block's (2014) call for attending to multimodality in applied linguistics research. Block emphasises the role of embodiment and multimodality in applied linguistics since they are vital for shaping our understanding of communication and meaning-making processes. Hence, MCA affords researchers in achieving an understanding of the complexity of classroom talk (Tai and Brandt, 2018; Tai and Khabbazbashi, 2019a; 2019b). Moreover, MCA is proved as an efficient tool for analysts to document the interactional norms, such as the norm of language alternation, that speakers orient to in interaction. The sequential analysis can allow analysts to identify how and when the classroom participant's uses of linguistic, multimodal, and spatial resources are appropriate or not in a given context (Bonacina-Pugh, 2012).

In Chapter 5, I have also demonstrated how the combination of MCA with IPA can shed light on the complexities of translanguaging practices and the sociocultural factors that affect teachers' meaning-making resources. It has been argued that MCA insists on revealing the details of talk in order to uncover how the interaction unfolds

(Schegloff, 1987). Such a perspective of context has been argued as being too narrow (e.g., Waring and Hruska, 2011; Waring et al., 2012; Matsumoto, 2018). By triangulating MCA with ethnographic details that are obtained from interview data or fieldnotes, it can strengthen the analysis and offer explanations of particular findings. Translanguaging practices are complex in nature since different sociocultural factors, including the speaker's personal history, life experience, identity, and beliefs, can affect their deployment of meaning-making resources in the process of constructing meanings. I have shown that triangulating MCA analysis with ethnographic information, particularly video-stimulated-recall-interview data, is helpful for analysts to understand the complexities of EMI teachers' translanguaging practices.

In Chapters 4 and 5, I have illustrated the ways researchers can employ the analytic framework of IPA to illuminate the 'insider' accounts (Smith et al., 2013) of the teachers' interpretations of their translanguaging practices in the lessons (Tai and Li, 2020, 2021a, 2021b, 2021c, 2023; Tai, 2022a, 2022b, 2023a, 2023b; Tai and Wong, 2022). I have demonstrated that using IPA allows researchers to take an emic approach in order to explore how the EMI teachers understand and make sense of their translanguaging practices in the classrooms. Combining MCA with IPA resonates with the methodological framework of moment analysis (Li, 2011; see Chapter 5), which requires researchers to collect video or audio recording of naturally occurring interactions and metalanguaging data. Hence, allowing the teachers to review their teaching practices during video-stimulated-recall interviews can help researchers to analyse the process of the teachers trying to articulate their perspectives of their own pedagogical practices. It also requires the researchers to move away from doing structural linguistic analysis for identifying the frequent and regular patterns. This redirects the researcher's focus on how language users utilise multilingual, multimodal, multisemiotic, and multisensory resources in particular moments of the classroom interactions and what may have resulted in a particular action at that specific moment.

6.2 Future Directions for Research in Applied Linguistics and Language Education

First, it must be noted that the findings generated from the combination of MCA and IPA (Chapter 5, Tai and Li, 2020, 2021a, 2021b, 2021c) cannot be generalised to other EMI classroom contexts given the contextualised nature of the study. The teacher's translanguaging practices may differ in other grades, other subject areas, or in other

EMI schools. Although the findings cannot be generalised to other contexts due to the central role of the specific context under study, what an MCA analysis provides is not empirical but analytical generalisation (Yin, 2009; Tai, 2022a), where each interactional feature is evidence that 'the machinery for its production is culturally available, involves members' competencies, and is therefore possible (and probably) reproducible' (Psathas, 1995: 50). That is, the findings are likely to be generalisable as descriptions of what other teachers can do in other classroom contexts, given the similar array of interactional and linguistic competencies as the students in this study. Moreover, instead of its generalisability, the findings aim to reveal the complexity of translanguaging practices in EMI classrooms. Particularly, through triangulating the MCA analysis with video-stimulated-recall-interview data, I am able to project multiple realities that may occur in translanguaging practices depending on different perspectives available from the teachers.

For reporting purposes, researchers can only select the representative extracts instead of presenting all the transcribed instances of teachers' translanguaging practices, due to the nature of micro-analysis of classroom interactions, which requires researchers to offer a detailed examination of sequences of interaction. Hence, such a method imposes a limit on the amount of data that are manageable to a single researcher in order to prevent compromising the quality of the micro-analysis. In order to address this concern, the following aspects are considered:

1 the presented extracts being directly or indirectly comparable to other extracts (ten Have, 1990);
2 the deviant cases being considered (Ford, 2012).

As ten Have (1990) argues, regardless of a single-case (i.e., one particular extract) analysis or collections of instances (similar or different), MCA analysis 'is always comparative, either directly or indirectly' (ten Have, 1990: 34). That is, the analysed extracts are interrelated to illustrate how the interactional features recurrently occur (by relevantly similar instances) or how the features are employed in dissimilar ways (by deviant instances). Additionally, based on my classroom observation, I select and transcribe the 'critical moments' or 'a point of significant, an instant when things change' (Pennycook, 2004: 330) particularly related to the teachers' translanguaging practices. In this regard, the research study should focus on the quality of the MCA transcriptions and analysis of 'critical' moments of teachers' translanguaging phenomena, instead of prioritising the amount of data transcription and analysis.

Alternatively, I do not offer any quantitative data that shows the correlation between the teachers' use of translanguaging in the EMI classrooms and the outcome of the students' content subject performance. In order to establish the efficacy of a translanguaging pedagogy for content and language learning purposes, future research can also include students' assessment data in order to closely examine the link between the teachers' translanguaging practices and the students' development of content and language acquisition. The quantitative evidence can potentially complement and triangulate the MCA analysis. This could result in valuable insights regarding how the affordances of the teachers' translanguaging practices are transferable to the student's academic learning outcomes.

Furthermore, it is possible that the teachers' translanguaging practices may not be always understood and accepted by all students within the classrooms. Therefore, it is worth investigating how translanguaging can exclude those who find themselves unable to participate in the classroom interaction for different reasons.

Lastly, I hope that more longitudinal case studies will be conducted by examining the affordances of translanguaging by different teachers in different linguistically and culturally diverse classrooms and subject areas. Researchers can draw on the combination of MCA and IPA for exploring teachers' translanguaging practices in achieving the specific pedagogical goals. This can enrich our understanding of how using translanguaging can lead to positive or negative outcomes on students' content acquisition and second language development.

References

Block, D. 2014. 'Moving beyond "lingualism": Multilingual embodiment and multimodality in SLA'. In S. May (ed.), *The multilingual turn: Implications for SLA, TESOL and bilingual education*. New York; London: Routledge. 54–77.

Bonacina-Pugh, F. 2012. 'Researching "practiced language policies": Insights from conversation analysis'. *Language Policy* 11 (3): 213–234.

Ford, C. 2012. 'Clarity in applied and interdisciplinary conversation analysis'. *Discourse Studies* 14: 507–513.

Jefferson, G. 2004. 'Glossary of transcript symbols with an introduction'. In G. Lerner (ed.), *Conversation analysis: Studies from the first generation*. Philadelphia: John Benjamins. 14–31.

Li, W. 2011. 'Moment analysis and translanguaging space: Discursive construction of identities by multilingual Chinese youth in Britain'. *Journal of Pragmatics* 43: 1222–1235.

Matsumoto, Y. 2018. 'At challenging but "learning" moments: Roles of nonverbal interactional resources for dealing with conflicts in English as a lingua franca classroom interactions'. *Linguistics and Education* 48: 35–51.

Mondada, L. 2018. 'Multiple temporalities of language and body in interaction: Challenges for transcribing multimodality'. *Research on Language and Social Interaction* 51 (1): 85–106.

Pennycook, A. 2004. 'Critical moments in a TESOL praxicum'. In B. Norton and K. Toohey (eds.), *Critical pedagogies and language learning*. Cambridge: Cambridge University Press. 327–346.

Psathas, G. 1995. *Conversation analysis: The study of talk-in-interaction*. Thousand Oaks, CA: Sage.

Schegloff, E. 1987. 'Some sources of misunderstanding in talk-in-interaction'. *Linguistics* 25 (1): 201–218.

Smith, J. A., P. Flowers., and M. Larkin. 2013. *Interpretative phenomenological analysis: Theory, method, and research*. Los Angeles, CA: Sage.

Tai, K. W. H. 2022a. 'Translanguaging as inclusive pedagogical practices in English medium instruction science and mathematics classrooms for linguistically and culturally diverse students'. *Research in Science Education* 52: 975–1012.

Tai, K. W. H. 2022b. 'A translanguaging perspective on teacher contingency in Hong Kong English medium instruction history classrooms'. *Applied Linguistics*. Epub ahead of print. https://doi.org/10.1093/applin/amac039

Tai, K. W. H. 2023a. 'Managing classroom misbehaviours in the Hong Kong English medium instruction secondary classrooms: A translanguaging perspective'. *System* 113: 1–35.

Tai, K. W. H. 2023b. 'Cross-curricular connection in an Hong Kong English medium instruction western history classroom: A translanguaging view'. *Language and Education*. Epub ahead of print. https://doi.org/10.1080/09500782.2023.2174379

Tai, K. W. H. and A. Brandt. 2018. 'Creating an imaginary context: Teacher's use of embodied enactments in addressing learner's initiatives in a beginner-level adult ESOL classroom'. *Classroom Discourse* 9 (3): 244–266.

Tai, K. W. H. and N. Khabbazbashi. 2019a. 'The mediation and organisation of gestures in vocabulary instructions: A microgenetic analysis of interactions in a beginning-level adult ESOL classroom'. *Language and Education* 33 (5): 445–468.

Tai, K. W. H. and N. Khabbazbashi. 2019b. 'Vocabulary explanations in beginning-level adult ESOL classroom interactions: A conversation analysis perspective'. *Linguistics and Education* 52: 61–77.

Tai, K. W. H. and W. Li. 2020. 'Bringing the outside in: Connecting students' out-of-school knowledge and experience through translanguaging in Hong Kong English medium instruction mathematics classes'. *System* 95: 1–32.

Tai, K. W. H. and W. Li. 2021a. 'Constructing playful talk through translanguaging in the English medium instruction mathematics classrooms'. *Applied Linguistics* 42 (4): 607–640.

Tai, K. W. H. and W. Li 2021b. 'Co-learning in Hong Kong English medium instruction mathematics secondary classrooms: A translanguaging perspective'. *Language and Education* 35 (3): 241–267.

Tai, K. W. H. and W. Li 2021c. 'The affordances of iPad for constructing a technology-mediated space in Hong Kong English medium instruction secondary classrooms: A translanguaging view'. *Language Teaching Research*. Epub ahead of print. https://doi.org/10.1177/136216882110278

Tai, K. W. H. and W. Li. 2023. 'Embodied enactment of a hypothetical scenario in an English medium instruction secondary mathematics classroom: A translanguaging approach'. *Language Teaching Research*. Epub ahead of print. https://doi.org/10.1093/applin/amac069

Tai, K. W. H. and C. Y. Wong. 2022. 'Empowering students through the construction of a translanguaging space in an English as a first language classroom'. *Applied Linguistics*. Epub ahead of print. https://doi.org/10.1093/applin/amac069

ten Have, P. 1990. 'Methodological issues in conversation analysis'. *Bulletin de Méthodologie Sociologique* 27: 23–51.

Waring, H. Z., S. Creider., T. Tarpey., and R. Black. 2012. 'A search for specificity in understanding CA and context'. *Discourse Studies*, 14 (4), 477–492.

Waring, H. Z. and B. L. Hruska. 2011. 'Getting and keeping Nora on board: A novice elementary ESOL student teacher's practices for lesson engagement'. *Linguistics and Education* 22: 441–455.

Yin, R. K. 2009. *Case study research: Design and methods* (4th ed.). London: SAGE Publications.

Appendix

Multimodal Conversation Analysis Transcription Conventions (Adapted from Jefferson, 2004, and Mondada, 2018)

Sequential and Timing Elements of the Interaction

[		Beginning point of simultaneous speaking (of two of more people)
]		End point of simultaneous speaking
=		Talk by two speakers which is contiguous
	OR	(i.e., not overlapping, but with no hearable pause in between)
		continuation of the same turn by the same speaker even though the turn is separated in the transcript
(0.2)		The time (in tenths of a second) between utterances
(.)		A micro-pause (one tenth of a second or less)

Paralinguistic Elements of Interaction

wo:rd	Sound extension of a word (more colons: longer stretches)
word.	Fall in tone (not necessarily the end of a sentence)
word,	Continuing intonation (not necessarily between clauses)
wor-	An abrupt stop in articulation
word?	Rising inflection (not necessarily a question)
wo<u>r</u>d	(underline) Emphasised word, part of word, or sound
word↑	Rising intonation
word↓	Falling intonation
°word°	Talk that is quieter than surrounding talk
hh	Audible out-breaths
.hh	Audible in-breaths

w(hh)ord   Laughter within a word
>word<   Talk that is spoken faster than surrounding talk
<word>   Talk that is spoken slower than surrounding talk
$word$ Talk uttered in a 'smile voice'

Other Conventions

(word)	Approximations of what is heard
((comment))	Analyst's notes
#	Indicating the exact locations of the figures in the transcripts
+	Marks the onset of a nonverbal action (e.g., shift of gaze, pointing)
XX	Inaudible utterances
--->	The action described continues across subsequent lines
--->+	The action described ends

Index

Pages in *italics* refer figures and **bold** refer tables.

Allard, E. 23
Applied Linguistics 1, 4–5, 13–14, 42, 107–109

Bagga-Gupta, S. 10
Becker, A. L. 10
bilingualism 9, 15–16
Black, R. 71
Block, D. 14, 106
Blommaert, J. 16
Bonacina-Pugh, F. 34–35

Charalambous, C. 23
Charalambous, P. 23
Collins, J. 16
content and language integrated learning (CLIL) 3, *4*, 20–21, 44, 101–102
content-based immersion (CBI) 3, *4*
Conversation Analysis (CA) 34–35; basic principles of 35–36
COVID-19 pandemic 60
Creider, S. 71

data analysis procedures: data analysis 41–42; identifying translanguaging instances 39–40; transcription of classroom interaction data 40–41
data collection method 2
discourse analysis (DA) 18, 20–21, 25
Discursive Psychology 61

Doiz, A. 20
double hermeneutic 52, 55, 60, 66
dynamic bilingualism 9, 16

Economic and Social Research Council (ESRC) 74
English-as-a-second-language 10
English as the academic purpose (EAP) 3, *4*
English as the specific purpose (ESP) 3
English medium instruction (EMI) 2, 4, 7, 66; classrooms 25, 67–69, 72–73, 101, 107–108; history classroom 85–100; mathematics classroom 75–85; teachers 25, 68, 85; teachers' complexities 107
ESRC-funded doctoral project: co-learning in an EMI history classroom 85–100; EMI mathematics classroom 75–85; linguistic ethnographic investigation 74; translanguaging practices 74
ethnographic data 47, 69–70

Finch, K. 59
first pair part (FPP) 37–38
Flowers, P. 53, 58
Ford, C. E. 38

García, O. 8, 10, 12
Gibson, J. L. 59
Gynne, A. 10

Heidegger, M. 54
He, P. 22
Heritage, J. 33
Ho, J. W. Y. 26
Hong Kong (HK) 65–103
Howard, K. B. 59
Ho, W. Y. J. 60
Husserl, E. 53–54
Hutchby, I. 40

Indian English accent 80, 84–85
interpretative phenomenological analysis (IPA) 1–2, 19; combination of MCA with 69–71, *70*, 109; data collection and analysis procedures 57–58, 72–73; hermeneutics 54–56; idiography 56–57; investigate multilingual practices in classrooms 59–60; limitations 61; phenomenology 53–54; theoretical and methodological frameworks of 52–53
IPA *see* interpretative phenomenological analysis

Jefferson, G. 37, 40, 106
Jewitt, C. 14

Kasper, G. 39
Katsos, N. 59
Kress, G. 13

L1/L2 dichotomisation 9
language education 5, 107–109
Lantolf, J. P. 14
Larkin, M. 53, 58
Lasagabaster, D. 20
Lefebvre, H. 17
Li., G. 25, 36
Lin, A. M. Y. 20, 42, 44
linguistic ethnographers 35
Li, W 8, 12–13, 15, 17–18, 21, 26, 59, 66–68
Love, Nigel 11

Macaro, E. 3
Makalela, L. 24
Marsh, D. 3
MCA *see* multimodal conversation analysis

MFL *see* modern foreign languages
modern foreign languages (MFL) 59
Mondada, L. 37, 40, 106
Moore, P. 20
multilingual classroom 2, 8; monolingual policy in 9
multilingual education programmes 2–4, *4*, 15
multilingualism 4, 8–9, 12, 15–17, 19–20, 59–60, 62
multimodal conversation analysis (MCA) 1–2, 19; analysis of translanguaging 73; analysis with ethnographic information 107; classroom interactions 36–37; combination of IPA with 69–71, 106; data analysis procedures 39–42; language policies 34; limitations 46–47; linguistic framework 35; multimodal phenomena in the transcripts 37; social interactions 37–39; talk-in-interaction 36
multimodality 4, 9, 13–15, 42, *101*, 102, 106
multi-scalar organisation 12

Nikula, T. 20

Osborn, M. 52, 61

phenomenological attitude 53
phenomenological reduction 54
plurilingualism 15

Richards, K. 33, 42
R. Wooffitt 40

Sacks, H. 37
Sah, P. 25
Schegloff, E. 37
Schegloff, E. A. 71
second-order language 12
second pair part (SPP) 37–38
Seedhouse, P. 39, 71
Serratrice, L. 59
Shohamy, E. 34
Slembrouck, S. 16
Smith, J. A. 52–58, 61

Smotrova, T. 14
social interactions: adjacency pairs 37–38; repair 38–39; turn-taking 38
Speer, N. 57
Swain, M. 10–11

Tai, K. W. H. 59–60, 66–68
talking-it-through 11
Tarpey, T. 71
ten Have, P. 108
Theakston, A. 59
Thibault, P. J. 11
Thompson, S. A. 38
transition-relevance places (TRP) 38
translanguaging 1, 7; analytical perspective and moment analysis 65–68; ecological psychology perspective of languaging 11–13; ethnographic approach 21–24; functional discourse analysis 20–21; mixed methods 24–26; multilingual classrooms 42–46; multimodality 13–15; pedagogical model 101; principles of classroom 18–19; sociocultural perspective of languaging 10–11; space 17
turn-construction units (TCUs) 38

van Lier, L. 39
video-stimulated-recall interview 81, **95**, 107; data 57

Wang, D. 18
Wantanabe, Y. 10
Waring, H. Z. 71
Williams, C. 7, 15
Willig, C. 61
Wong, C. Y. 67
Woodley, H. H. 20
Wu., Y. 20, 42, 44

Zembylas, M. 23

For Product Safety Concerns and Information please contact our EU representative GPSR@taylorandfrancis.com
Taylor & Francis Verlag GmbH, Kaufingerstraße 24, 80331 München, Germany

www.ingramcontent.com/pod-product-compliance
Lightning Source LLC
Chambersburg PA
CBHW051754230426
43670CB00012B/2288